Serving
the Word

Elements of Preaching

O. Wesley Allen Jr., series editor

Thinking Theologically
The Preacher as Theologian
Ronald J. Allen

Knowing the Context
Frames, Tools, and Signs for Preaching
James R. Nieman

Interpreting the Bible
Approaching the Text in Preparation for Preaching
Mary F. Foskett

Shaping the Claim
Moving from Text to Sermon
Marvin A. McMickle

Determining the Form
Structures for Preaching
O. Wesley Allen Jr.

Finding Language and Imagery
Words for Holy Speech
Jennifer L. Lord

Delivering the Sermon
Voice, Body, and Animation in Proclamation
Teresa L. Fry Brown

Serving the Word
Preaching in Worship
Melinda A. Quivik

Serving the Word

Preaching in Worship

Melinda A. Quivik

Fortress Press
Minneapolis

Cover image: © iStockphoto.com/Igor Skrynnikov
Cover and book design: John Goodman

Library of Congress Cataloging-in-Publication Data
Quivik, Melinda A. (Melinda Ann)
Serving the Word : preaching in worship / Melinda A. Quivik.
    p. cm. — (Elements of preaching)
Includes bibliographical references (p.   ).
ISBN 978-0-8006-6198-4 (alk. paper)
1. Liturgical preaching. 2. Lectionary preaching. I. Title.
BV4235.L58Q58 2009
251—dc22
                                        2009026334

The paper used in this publication meets the minimum requirements of American National
Standard for Information Sciences—Permanence of Paper for Printed Library Materials,
ANSI Z329.48-1984.

Manufactured in the U.S.A.

13   12   11   10   09   1   2   3   4   5   6   7   8   9   10

Contents

Editor's Foreword

Preparing beginning preachers to stand before the body of Christ and proclaim the word of God faithfully, authentically, and effectively Sunday after Sunday is and always has been a daunting responsibility. As North American pastors face pews filled with citizens of a postmodern, post-Christendom culture, this teaching task becomes even more complex. The theological, exegetical, and homiletical skills that preachers need for the future are as much in flux today as they have ever been in Western Christianity. Thus providing seminary students with a solid but flexible homiletical foundation at the start of their careers is a necessity.

Traditionally, professors of preaching choose a primary introductory textbook that presents a theology of proclamation and a process of sermon development and delivery from a single point of view. To maintain such a singular point of view is the sign of good writing, but it does at times cause problems for learning in pluralistic settings. One approach to preaching does not fit all. Yet a course simply surveying all of the homiletical possibilities available will not provide a foundation on which to build either.

Furthermore, while there are numerous introductory preaching textbooks from which to choose, most are written from the perspective of Euro-American males. Classes supplement this view with smaller homiletical texts written by women and persons of color. But a pedagogical hierarchy is nevertheless set up: the white male voice provides the main course and women and persons of color provide the side dishes.

Elements of Preaching is a series designed to help professors and students of preaching—including established preachers who want to develop their skills in specific areas—construct a sound homiletical foundation in a conversational manner. This conversation is meant to occur at two levels. First, the series as a whole deals with basic components found in most introductory preaching classes: theology of proclamation, homiletical contexts, biblical interpretation, sermonic claim, language and imagery, rhetorical form, delivery, and worship. But each element is presented by a different scholar, all of whom represent diversity in terms of gender, theological traditions (Baptist, Disciple of Christ, Lutheran, Presbyterian, and United Methodist), and ethnicity (African American, Asian American, and Euro-American). Instead of bringing in different voices at the margin of the preaching class, Elements of Preaching creates a conversation around the central topics of an introductory course without foregoing essential instruction concerning sermon construction and embodiment. Indeed, this level of conversation is extended beyond the printed volumes through the Web site www.ElementsofPreaching.com.

Second, the individual volumes are written in an open-ended manner. The individual author's particular views are offered but in a way that invites, indeed demands, the readers to move beyond them in developing their own approaches to the preaching task. The volumes offer theoretical and practical insights, but at the last page it is clear that more must be said. Professors and students have a solid place to begin, but there is flexibility within the class (and after the class in ministry) to move beyond these volumes by building on the insights and advice they offer.

In this volume, Melinda A. Quivik introduces readers to the ways in which the sermon does (or should) relate to the whole of the worship service. Too often, seminary courses in liturgy and in preaching give students the impression that preparation for preaching and planning the liturgy and music are separate tasks. Quivik effectively shows how proclamation and table, prayers and congregational song can (and should) all serve the word of God as offered in the Scripture readings for the day. This service to the word is unpacked in two primary ways. First, she reminds readers that while the Protestant Church often worships in a pattern in which everything revolves around the sermon, the ancient pattern of the dual foci of word and table better evokes the mystery of God's good news. Second, she shows how each of the four broad movements of most Christian worship practices (Gathering, Word, Table, Sending or Gathering, Word, Response, Sending) serve the word broadly and relate to the sermon specifically. Readers of *Serving the Word* will no longer be able to go about the Monday through Saturday work of preparing for worship thinking about preaching *and* worship but will always, in a more healthy and effective manner, think about preaching *in* worship.

O. Wesley Allen Jr.

Introduction

The title of this book, *Serving the Word,* carries a helpful double meaning. To serve the word is both *to receive* and *to offer* it. On the one hand, receiving takes place when people gather to hear God's word proclaimed through reading the Bible and preaching. The Risen Christ speaks to us as the face of God, present in our midst through the word. In all its forms, the word of God is proclaimed in the liturgy. That proclamation is, certainly, reading and preaching, but it is also the people's proclamation in song and prayer.

Offering the word, on the other hand, is first what God has done: given to us in the imagery, narratives, poetry, pleading, hymns, stories, characters, landscapes, dreams, visions, and more that inhabit the Holy Scriptures. But serving the word is also what the church does by making sure that the word is in our midst week after week. In our coming together, listening, proclaiming, eating, and being sent out again, the word of God is served by the body of Christ. God's word serves God's people and God's people serve the word.

Liturgical theologian Gordon Lathrop addresses the pervasive nature of the scriptural word as it finds expression throughout the liturgy:

> The Bible marks and largely determines Christian corporate worship. It is fair to say that the liturgies of the diverse churches all have a biblical character. . . . [A]t the heart of the meeting the Bible is read and then interpreted as having to do with us. . . . Furthermore, the text of the Bible provides the source of the imagery and, often, the very form and quality of the language in prayers, chants, hymn texts, and sermons. Psalms are sung as if that ancient collection were intended for our singing. Snatches of old biblical letters are scattered throughout the service, as if we were addressed. Frequently images and texts drawn from the Bible adorn the room where the meeting takes place. To people who know the biblical stories, the very actions of the gathering may seem like the Bible alive: an assembly gathers, as the people gathered at the foot of Mount Sinai, the holy convocation of the Lord; arms are upraised in prayer or blessing, as Moses raised his arms; the holy books are read, as Ezra read to the listening people; the people hold a meal, as the disciples

1

did, gathered after the death of Jesus. To come into the meeting seems like
coming into a world determined by the language of the Bible.[1]

The word of God founds, guides, and animates all of worship. *Proclamation of the word in the sermon serves the whole of the worship just as the
worship serves the preaching.* This is the subject of this book.

In order to see how this serving occurs, we will look at some recent
work by liturgical scholars. Especially since the mid-twentieth century,
scholars have written about an ecumenical worship pattern evident
through the two millennia since Jesus' time and across denominations.
The pattern is plain in Luke's story of Jesus' postresurrection appearance
on the road to Emmaus and at the table (Luke 24:13-35). It contains a complete image of the ecumenical pattern: gathering as two become three
on the road, Jesus opening the scriptures to the disciples, Jesus breaking
the bread through which his identity gives new vision, and the disciples
leaving to find the others. We will explore these parts in detail in coming
chapters. In the Emmaus pattern of Gathering, Word, Meal (or Response),
and Sending, the relationship between preaching and worship as separate
aspects of liturgical experience breaks down. Preaching and the breaking
of bread are intimately connected. The word of God explained by the
stranger on the road becomes, around the table at Emmaus, suddenly
revealed as a "burning" in the heart. The disciples' eyes are opened when
the word is linked to the bread.

Other books in the Elements of Preaching series place the preaching
task under a microscope, as it were, in order to unpack the various pieces
of the sermon from preparation through delivery. This book will invite the
reader to see how God's word is the crux not only of preaching but also
of the worship service as a whole, that the whole liturgy serves the Word
as Christ is revealed in the midst of God's holy people.

The liturgy in its totality offers the assembly multiple ways to enter into
the word, enriching the sermon by stretching its scope. Likewise, the liturgy
is served by the preached word of God as it articulates particular biblical
themes, makes tangible the abstractions, and invites local cultural expectations to inform the sermon. At the heart of both the sermon and the rest
of the liturgy, God's word, the Bible, holds open its merciful visions.

This book contends that a liturgical experience grounded in—and
shaped by—the word of God as it is preached in the context of Word-
centered worship has the capacity to address the needs of people in every

age. For some people, this contention may seem dated, too tied to "tradition," fraught with hierarchical decision-making structures. The technological changes of our time raise questions about the ways in which people receive information, ideas, impressions, experiences, and feelings. When we speak of word in worship, what sort of "word" are we talking about? Is word static or can it be in motion, electric with emphasis? Is word also image? Or does word contain image as one medium through which ideas are manifested? Is word quick enough to hold our attention any longer? Do we have the patience to listen to the word? Do we have the capacity any longer to enter into a narrative for a sustained period of time as our ancestors did? Can we take Mary's place at Jesus' feet? Or does word demand to be presented in flexible, shifting lights in order to hold us and capture our imaginations? People who spend time in a virtual world are used to being confronted with a number of different ways in which thoughts are represented and with rapid movement from one form to another.[2]

Liturgical leaders and planners best serve the assembly's worship by placing the scriptural texts at the heart of the liturgy. When all aspects of the liturgy are grounded in the word of God for the day—whatever media are used—a certain cohesion of impression resounds. The word becomes the glue for all that occurs whether mediated through music, art, spoken and sung word, or other technology. The assembly does not grasp the meaning of God's word simply by cognitive means but by living within many modes of expression: verbal and nonverbal, spoken and silent, still and moving, through symbols presented and even through their absence.

Every Sunday the biblical texts differ from the previous week. Over time, many texts are proclaimed. When God's word is the core of the worship, the assembly sees the Lord and itself in the light of that word, through God's lens. Images and themes address or exemplify the word of God for that day and bring together even conflicting interpretations that locate the worshipers in the multivalent complex of God's reign. Because the preached word and the liturgical event within which preaching is located are integral to each other, this book invites the reader to explore how—through God's word—the worship event as a whole informs and, in turn, supports preaching.

Liturgy, Pattern, and Practice

Before we enter into this exploration, a few preliminary explanations are in order. First, *liturgy* is what is done in the course of the Sunday assembly.

No church's worship event is devoid of liturgy. The words *worship* and *liturgy* will be used interchangeably here. To speak of a "liturgical church" is really to refer to all churches. Whatever the worship looks like, it is a liturgy (*leitourgia*). Scholars disagree about whether *leitourgia* ought to be translated "the work of the people."[3] A *leitourgia* in Roman times was a form of "public service" and seems to have been used both for the wealthy to display their generosity in order to gain more power and for the ministry of priests or those who performed charitable acts. What people commonly mean by "liturgical" does not constitute liturgical worship. In common parlance, "liturgical" usually refers to parts of the liturgy that are present almost every week such as the greeting or dialog ("The Lord be with you." "And also with you") or the song sung at Holy Communion ("Holy, holy, holy, Lord, God of power and might . . ."). These are responses, hymns, invitations using scriptural language to anchor the worship in the Bible. To understand better that liturgy is a pattern rather than the language or song that repeats each week, it is good to keep in mind that every assembly practices its liturgy.

Every denomination and every church has a *pattern* to its worship. That pattern is "the liturgy" of that denomination or congregation. For Protestants, the liturgy takes diverse forms, including both Holy Communion and what is called "ante-communion" or a Service of the Word. For evangelicals, it is often joyous singing, a pastor's prayer, reading the word and preaching, intercessory prayer, and an altar call. So-called Praise and Worship services are liturgical in that they follow a pattern each week very close to the pattern just named. For many Quakers, the liturgy is sitting in silence until, at a certain point, someone rises to speak of what has come to her or him. This is a form of response to the word that is "heard" in silence. For Roman Catholics, the liturgy is the mass of Holy Communion. Orthodox churches speak of "the divine liturgy" that is continuously ongoing in the heavenly realm and which a given assembly participates in through ancient chant, incense, preaching, and the meal.

Diverse ecclesial practices also influence the liturgy of a denomination or a congregation. Where clergy ordination is a requirement for presiding at the meal, churches have altered practices to accord with availability of pastors and priests. For many Protestants, frontier settlement in the United States required churches to abandon the weekly meal because there were not enough clergy to preside. Especially for these denominations, the liturgical renewal movement has encouraged the use of weekly communion in order that the churches might experience practices lost due to historical realities. Where laity lead services (Mennonites and Disciples of Christ, among others), the availability of ordained Christians did not influence the shape of the liturgy. For the black church, with roots in secret gatherings under the horrible oppression of slavery—where worship was a time for regaining dignity, singing hope, giving courage and comfort—the liturgical pattern is grounded in celebration. Cultural realities not only inform the shape and content of worship but also play a role in determining ecclesial structures and, ultimately, doctrine.

The task for worship planners and leaders in every denomination and congregation is to be aware of the influences of culture in order to weigh and test its potential transformation of the faith. Does the liturgical shape, for example, serve the preaching or does it mimic cultural expectations without regard for doctrine? Does the preaching serve the larger message of the liturgy or does it undermine the content of the confession of sin and of faith, the meanings offered through the hymns, the very content of the gathering? These are not easy questions to answer but must be kept in the forefront of worship critique.

Worship and preaching are concerned equally with theory and practice. In chapters 1 and 2, the theory of God's word as central to worship and of worship serving an ancient pattern will be discussed. Chapter 3 looks at an Ash Wednesday worship in order to use it throughout the rest of the book as a specific example of the ways in which preaching and worship influence each other. Chapters 4 through 7 cover the parts of the liturgy in greater detail.

A Few Notes on Language

First, some quotations from older sources in these chapters include non-gender-inclusive pronouns for God and for humans beings. I have left them as the author wrote them. I assume that readers will graciously understand the distance scholars have moved in recent decades toward acknowledgment of inappropriate pronouns and also gendered names for God who is beyond gender identity.

Second, the term *Sunday assembly* refers to the regular weekly worship of the churches. Many churches, of course, meet at other times during the week, but Christians have held to the Sunday meeting since the beginning. The word *assembly* includes those who are believers and those who may not be able to articulate why they are attending. In short, it includes everyone assembled, not just church members or the baptized.

Third, there is a certain ambiguity to the term *word*, which will be discussed further in chapter 1. In general, where *word* refers clearly to the Risen Christ, it will be capitalized (Word). Where *word* is lowercased, it refers to the biblical text and also to the presence of Christ available to the congregation through the reading and preaching.

Chapter 1

God's Word Is Central in Worship

Preaching serves the liturgy and the liturgy serves preaching because both are founded in the word of God. When faced with a mystery as huge as life and death, human beings seek a stable and sure foundation from which to survey the landscape. God's word is reliable, sure, unswerving, a source of salvation. Words are, after all, visible on a page, rendering for all people a sense that this God is available. The words do not disappear when we close the book. At least until the next translation is published from the ancient languages, the words do not change.

Because God's word invites divergent interpretations, these complexities compel us to talk with each other about God's meaning. Conversation about scriptural interpretation takes place in an atmosphere of intense conviction, testifying to the importance of God's word in the lives of God's people. Christians would not be so heated over doctrine and worship—would not split off so vehemently from each other—if what God's word says for us did not matter. By the same token, we would not be drawn to each other with the tenderness and commitment visible in congregations and between churches everywhere if we did not find in God's word the very center of our life together. Because we see it as central, we are united by the word of God.

What is meant by God's word, however, is much bigger than the words on a page. God's word is not only the Holy Scriptures—the biblical canon—but also Word of God: Jesus of Nazareth, the Risen One, the Christ, holy revelation, presence of God, source of redemption. Word is also preaching, and in this sense God's word comes to us as both *word* and *Word*, for what is preached is the revelation of God in the midst of the world, a proclamation, a prophetic voice, a speaking that creates community by raising in the people's hearing the questions and assertions that lie at the heart of what puzzles and feeds us. Although the Bible does not contain a prescription for what worship ought to look like, we do have glimpses of the formative shape of worship on which the church is built. It is possible to imagine the structures and patterns of worship today echoing a number of biblical passages that highlight the fundamental importance of assembly, participation, and preaching the word. Notice the focus on gathering the people in Nehemiah 8:

> When the seventh month came—the people of Israel . . . told the scribe Ezra to bring the book of the law of Moses, which the LORD had given to Israel. . . . And Ezra opened the book in the sight of all the people, for he was standing above all the people; and when he opened it, all the people stood up. Then Ezra blessed the LORD, the great God, and all the people answered, "Amen, Amen," lifting up their hands. Then they bowed their heads and worshiped the LORD with their faces to the ground . . . (Neh. 7:73b—8:1, 5-6).

A number of stories in the New Testament show the early church gathered together in bewilderment, struggling to find its way, and praying. Whether the scriptural references describe actual gatherings or amalgamated events meant to offer a portrait of the church for a particular reason or for teaching is not critical to the impression they give or the information that can be gleaned from them. In the New Testament images of Christians at worship we see the church as a community, a body, comprised of more than a mere listing of individuals. The church's identity is corporate. The body of Christ, its self-understanding, and its theology are formed by its gathering.

While the church's worship patterns and practices are varied, the diversity need not divide the body of Christ. Rather, the diversity of worship patterns and practices show that differences between denominations— and even differences between churches within denominations—allow for a richer and therefore more complete understanding of God's presence among God's people. While we look at the common grounding in God's word among nearly all Christian worshipers and rejoice over the abundance of expressions, we can marvel at the centrality of participation by those who gather together, of reading Scripture and preaching, of prayer and prayer through song, of a meal, and of leave taking. We see, in effect, the pattern of Gathering to hear the Word, to eat a Meal, and to be Sent out.

A Participating Assembly

Participation serves preaching by providing each person the occasion to engage with God's word. Everyone has a role in worship. In 1 Corinthians Paul describes a worship gathering in which the mention of concrete offerings from individuals shows that the church's way of being together is based in what each one contributes.

> When you come together, each one has a hymn, a lesson, a revelation, a tongue, or an interpretation. Let all things be done for building up. If anyone speaks in a tongue, let there be only two or at most three, and each in turn; and let one interpret. But if there is no one to interpret, let them be silent in church and speak to themselves and to God. Let two or three prophets speak, and let the others weigh what is said. If a revelation is made to someone else sitting nearby, let the first person be silent. For you can all prophesy one by one, so that all may learn and all be encouraged . . . be eager to prophesy, and do not forbid speaking in tongues; but all things should be done decently and in order. (1 Cor. 14:26-31, 39-40)

This admonition is given to help the church learn how to worship. Note that this is not a prescription for what *ought* to happen in worship but a depiction of diverse contributions, word offerings, and the practice of weighing what is said.

The 1 Corinthians passage is about order and intention. Worship cannot nourish the people if it is chaotic. Worship is meant for "building up." The Greek word *oikodomēn* describes the church both as an "economy," a working relationship, and a domicile, a home. Everything that is included in worship should have a constructive purpose. First, we find variants of *oikodomēn* used as a noun: a building, such as temple buildings (Matt. 24:1); something that is constructed (Mark 12:10); a heavenly building that is promised when the earthly building is destroyed (2 Cor. 5:1); and in 1 Corinthians 3:9 the church is God's building.

Second, *oikodomēn* is used figuratively to refer to an activity that is edifying, that "builds up," as in the ongoing construction of communities made up of strengthened individuals. In this sense, *oikodomēn* refers to the many members and the responsibility of each to engage in conduct that is useful and faithful, encourages "those who prophesy [to] speak to other people for their upbuilding and encouragement" (1 Cor. 14:3), and how "Each of us must please our neighbor for the good purpose of building up the neighbor" (Rom. 15:2). While these uses of *oikodomēn* focus on the individual, other passages speak to the creation of the church as a body. In 2 Corinthians 12:19 and 13:10 the epistle writer urges building up the church. In Ephesians 2:21 the assembly and the building become one: "In him the whole structure is joined together and grows into a holy temple in the Lord."[1]

Having established the foundation of this "economic house" as a construction that encourages, shelters, and nourishes, individuals can expect to find themselves a part of a community built on certain principles. First, each person coming to worship brings an offering, a preparation, already having paid attention to the needs of the assembly. Second, limits are placed on how many people speak and what they say. Acknowledging that everyone will have a turn, this insistence on limitations recognizes the fundamental requirements of civility and boundaries. Not everyone should speak in tongues for as long as there is time, but only two or three. And only two or three prophets should speak. Those who are silent observers are to listen and be altered by it. Others will listen to determine what is of use and what is not. And finally, what is done must be sensible to the assembly. If the worship is conducted in an unfamiliar symbol-system, it must be translated. This can be applied to much more than simply words or utterances of "tongues." It can include spatial arrangements that are foreign or movements and gestures or songs and rhythms. If building up is the goal, and the course for doing that is the ready participation of the assembly, this text already points to central themes of liturgical renewal in our time.

Participation, then, requires gathering (bringing one's full faculties and offerings). Throughout Scripture the church is found praying and singing. By singing together, the church publicly proclaims its heart: "About midnight Paul and Silas were praying and singing hymns to God, and the prisoners were listening to them" (Acts 16:25). This is worship conducted in the face of oppression and despair. God's word comes into the midst of those who are unjustly confined and abused. While the church prays and sings, people who are not part of the church (or not yet!) witness a way of endurance and hope.

Glimpses of early Christian worship do not tell us, of course, the substance or thematic structure of hymns, readings, revelations, tongues, or interpretive choices. We do not know exactly in which order anything was or might have been done. We do know that the people were admonished to keep order and to pray and prophesy for the building up of the community. Liturgical action served the word.

Proclaiming and Preaching

Those who study preaching expect that God's word read and proclaimed will be part of worship. What do we learn about serving the word in Scripture? The story of Paul meeting with the church, presumably in Troas, surrounds the reading with a number of vital qualities that constitute the liturgical event even today.

> On the first day of the week [Sunday], when we met to break bread, Paul was holding a discussion with them; since he intended to leave the next day, he continued speaking until midnight. There were many lamps in the room upstairs where we were meeting. A young man named Eutychus, who was sitting in the window, began to sink off into a deep sleep while Paul talked still longer. Overcome by sleep, he fell to the ground three floors below and was picked up dead. But Paul went down, and bending over him took him in his arms, and said, "Do not be alarmed, for his life is in him." Then Paul went upstairs, and after he had broken bread and eaten, he continued to converse with them until dawn; then he left. (Acts 20:7-11)

This scene offers an image of how liturgy serves the preaching. Notice that the text says the gathering "met to break bread." The foundation of the gathering was food, although the sort of a meal is not clear. We cannot know whether the "discussion" was (1) proclamation of the word of God delivered by Paul as a preacher; (2) a debate over matters of interpretation; (3) a question-and-answer period with the apostle; (4) an evening of evangelizing toward greater stewardship and mission outreach; or (5) something else entirely. Yet the conjunction of word and meal is apparent. The substance of the gathering was so crucial that even Eutychus's near-death was not enough to break it up, pointing to the intensity and import of the exchange, the assembly's stretched abilities (how hard it is to stay awake through the night!), and the need for a leader.

In other words, the preaching is served by a leader whose urgent message is met by eager listeners who agree on a time to come together. The gathering offers food for the heart and mind and other food for the stomach.

Praying

Preaching is also served by prayer as both are permeated with God's word. In the very center of the Bible, we find the oldest hymnbook—the ancient prayers of the Hebrew people in the Psalms. Prayer has inexplicable necessity. God's people have practiced it in private and public, in search of personal revelation, in the desert, in print, through music and dance, by writing and by painting and conceiving icons, weaving and doing handwork, and in appeals to God's intervention for the public well-being. In the Psalms we see the full range of prayer concerns: lament and pleading, joyous thanksgiving, and honor toward the creator, savior, and advocate.

Intercessory prayer in worship is offered so that the church pours itself out to lift up to God the concerns and needs of the world. In Anne Lamott's famous schema, prayer is almost always "Thank you! Thank you! Thank you! Help me! Help me! Help me!"[2] This is not just the structure of an individual's prayer but also the church's. The assembly gives thanks to God for all things and then begs God's intervention and wisdom for the sake of the earth, for all people of faith, the nations, communities, and local concerns, often leaving time for the assembly to speak aloud or silently additional concerns and joys. The prayer of the people ends with a thanksgiving for the saints who have gone before.

Christians pray because God has commanded us to pray. We pray for our own communities but not before we have prayed for others. The prayers direct our attention to the many places where suffering needs to be met with deep compassion. In so doing, the word of God, so full of prayers, becomes our own words through Jesus Christ, in the Holy Spirit who groans within us even when we do not have the words ourselves.

Through prayer, God's word bridges distances and gives cohesion to the church when its members are not able to gather together in person. "While Peter was kept in prison, the church prayed fervently to God for him. . . . As soon as [Peter] realized [he was free from prison], he went to the house of Mary, the mother of John whose other name was Mark, where many had gathered and were praying" (Acts 12:5, 12). When Peter is released from prison by the help of what he comes to understand is an angel, he realizes that the Lord has rescued him, and he immediately goes to the place where the church is gathered in prayer. This story images a strong connection between the power of God's word to release us from our prisons and to bring us together in a new bond of freedom.

We also see in Scripture the gathered people responding throughout the worship with assent to the things they are hearing just as with the assembly gathered in Nehemiah 8 to hear the priest, Ezra, read. The response of the people is not only an ending to a prayer petition or response to prayer but a prayer of its own. The church in Corinth was given a way of understanding the reason for its assertion, "Amen," in this way: "For in [Christ Jesus] every one of God's promises is a 'Yes.' For this reason it is through him that we say the 'Amen,' to the glory of God." (2 Cor. 1:20). The church says "Amen" to the word of life and hope and in so doing establishes its cohesion. In some congregations, the "Amen" comes out as a unified voice; in others, individuals call it when the Holy Spirit urges a response. In all cases, the Amen is an affirmation of God's word at work in the present moment.

Prayer is also fundamental to the church's identity. In the story of Judas's betrayal and death, the apostles seek to replace him. Two names are put forward. "Then they prayed and said, 'Lord, you know everyone's heart. Show us which one of these two you have chosen to take the place in this ministry and apostleship from which Judas turned aside to go to his own place.' And they cast lots for them, and the lot fell on Matthias; and he was added to the eleven apostles" (Acts 1:24-26). God's word creates a context for the manipulation of decisive instruments (the lots). God's word is central to the church's reason for being, its discernment about direction, its leaders, and its patterns of work and worship.

Eating the Meal

Liturgical scholars have brought to our attention the ancient church's gathering around word *and* meal by which the followers of the Risen Christ kept their identity and retold their story. This is important to note, since the churches of North America have for many reasons and over a long period of time diminished use of this meal practice. (We will discuss the place of the meal in worship, through the story of Emmaus, in more detail in chapter 6.)

God's word gives us diverse accounts of Jesus' last supper (Matt. 26:26-29; Mark 14:22-25; Luke 22:15-20), including what Paul wrote to the church at Corinth:

For I received from the Lord what I also handed on to you, that the Lord Jesus on the night when he was betrayed took a loaf of bread, and when he had given thanks, he broke it and said, "This is my body that is for you. Do this in remembrance of me." In the same way he took the cup also, after supper, saying, "This cup is the new covenant in my blood. Do this, as often as you drink it, in remembrance of me." For as often as you eat this bread and drink the cup, you proclaim the Lord's death until he comes. (1 Cor. 11:23-25)

More than a prayer or an admonition, this meal offers a visible metaphor of how God's word works among the assembly: gathering the people to take in and digest what is simultaneously simple and profound, temporal and ultimate, encompassing past, present, and future. It is both proclamation of its own meaning as gift and command to remember Jesus *in* bread and wine.

Extrabiblical documents from the early church, unearthed in recent decades, contain glimpses of worship meals. The oldest, the *Didache*—from between 50 to 100 C.E.—was discovered in 1873.[3] Justin Martyr's *First Apology*,[4] written in 150 C.E., explains to Emperor Antoninus Pius (in power from 138 to 161) what Christians did and believed in order to persuade the emperor to stop persecuting them. From c. 315 C.E. we have the *Apostolic Tradition*,[5] which contains descriptions of ordination for bishops, presbyters, and deacons, including prayers that are said at such times, the orders for parts of the liturgy, and a detailed second part dealing with teaching newcomers the faith. We cannot know whether this document records the normal actions of the liturgy in order to teach it or is an attempt of the writer(s) to prescribe what should be done. Regardless, the influence of the document is seen in the fact that much of the language found in the ancient liturgy is still used in worship today.

Forming the Church

Some scholars now think that the *Didache* may have been written a mere twenty years or so after the crucifixion of Jesus of Nazareth and shortly before Paul wrote his epistles to the churches. It was certainly written in a political climate that was hostile to the church. The *Didache* (literally: The Training—or Teaching—of the Twelve Apostles) describes "the preserved oral tradition whereby mid-first-century house churches detailed the step-by-step transformation by which gentile converts were to be prepared for full active participation in their assemblies."[6]

The *Didache* seems to have served as a guide, then, for teaching the faith. It begins by establishing the "two ways: one of life and one of death," detailing the vast differences between them and the practices that build up the community, dealing with baptism in surprisingly precise terms, leaving more and more open the options for use of water. Best, it says, is immersion in a river. If that's not possible, use other water whether warm or cold.[7]

Whatever amount or kind of water is available, the *Didache* only insists that the water be poured three times invoking the name of the triune God. From the beginning, the church recognized that worship—even central sacramental moments—would need to be conducted differently from place to place, allowing for necessary inculturation. Only water itself and words naming the Trinity would be the same everywhere, and these elements could not be arbitrarily treated. However God's word is served, some core convictions transcend place while other aspects call for response to local options.

Regarding assembly on the Lord's Day, Sunday, the *Didache's* instruction assumes four things. The church gathers on "the day of the Lord" because (1) it is the day on which Christ Jesus was raised from the dead and it is God's own "divinely instituted" desire; (2) the church confesses sin when it gathers; (3) the church gives thanks; and (4) the church breaks bread.

A certain logic is expressed in this description of the fundamental actions in worship, just as there is a logic in the *Didache* itself. Prior to baptism, the church teaches the difference between the way of life and the way of death. Those who will be baptized learn the Ten Commandments and the Lord's Prayer. They learn about the orderliness of God's divine love for the world. They are baptized in water "in the name . . ." From then on, every Lord's day they gather with others to acknowledge sin, give thanks, and eat a meal.

The *Didache* admonishes and teaches the ways and times for fasting (on Wednesdays and Fridays, as distinct from the "pagans" who fast on Mondays and Thursdays)[8] and for prayer, especially the Lord's Prayer. But what it does not even mention is the practice of reading Scripture and preaching. What are we to make of this? Is it possible that this document may have left out some aspects of its general practices because they were so familiar they did not need to be mentioned?

Such is the case with much of contemporary practice. Our church orders and instructions, for instance, do not mention the need to turn on the lights when we gather or arrange the chairs. Those things are not worth mentioning because they are so necessary and everywhere practiced. Perhaps the writers of Didache, likewise, do not remark on the obvious parts of the liturgy such as reading the prophets and letters of the evangelist(s) and preaching.

Unlike the Didache, Justin Martyr's First Apology describes the preached word in quite particular terms: "On Sunday all who live in cities or in the country gather together to one place. The memoirs of the apostles or the writings of the prophets are read for as long as time allows. When the reader has ceased, the presider exhorts and invites us into the pattern of these good things."[9] Here is a portrait of a church struggling to make itself plain and nonthreatening to the oppressive powers. The preacher, to whom Justin refers as the "presider" (one who "presides," who calls the gathering and sets out the order for the time together) is also the preacher, the one who gives a discourse on the readings. The preacher calls the people into a pattern—to see themselves as having been given abundant life because of—the design of "these good things" that God has set out. Perhaps this gave the emperor a glimpse of how he might see his way to stop killing them! Christians might be allowed to live if all they do is listen to a reading and a speech, eat, and give to the needy. What could be less threatening?

Today the eucharistic ("thanksgiving") meal practices of Christians differ widely. Some omit the weekly meal described in the Didache, Justin's First Apology, and the Apostolic Tradition. When churches do not hold the communion meal, they practice instead a Service of the Word, also called "ante-communion" because the word comes before (ante-) the communion meal in the full Holy Communion liturgy. Speaking of a Service of the Word as one that is part of a longer pattern of word plus meal indicates that the "norm" is the latter. Of course, not all denominations or churches agree on what is the norm, but it is in fact the pattern we see in Justin's description: Gathering, Word, Meal, and Sending food and money to the poor.

When a meal is held, churches vary on the prayer said over the food. Some Christian churches today use a pattern much like the Didache, while others use a longer prayer based in early documents like the Apostolic Tradition that includes a recitation of thanks for creation, for Christ Jesus, remembering the words he said at the Last Supper, and for the Holy Spirit.

Some churches use only the Words of Institution (also called the *verba*) before distributing the meal, believing that Jesus' words are proclamation of the meaning of the bread and the wine and must stand alone. For them, the prayer said over the meal is not to be thanksgiving for all that God has done, but a declaration of the meaning of meal as in "This is my body . . . do this . . . ."

The discrepancy in words said over the meal serves to help us continually critique the bases of our own practices so that we hold in tension the valuable paradoxes that lie at the heart of God's word about this food of life. When Jesus took and blessed the bread and wine, his blessing can be understood as a thanksgiving in the classic Jewish pattern of *berakah*. Yet he also used the complicated verb of existence—"is"— to describe what he held in his hands to bless ("This is my body . . ."). The texts of the Last Supper, at minimum, direct us to understand the bread and wine in some way as Jesus' body and blood.

The church has been divided for two millennia over the meaning of that one word *is*. Do we say the elements both are and are not his body and blood or only one or the other? This disagreement is clear in the churches that were founded on the theologies of Rome (transubstantiation), Luther (real presence, ambiguity), Calvin (presence of Christ is in the gathered people), and Zwingli (we remember the historic Jesus in the meal). Do we say his words of blessing are thanksgiving or proclamation or both?

To find our unity as the church of Christ requires us to hold these differences in tension, appreciating the vast possibilities for the ways they show us greater complexity and great depth of faith. There is no one right way. But in all of them, the preaching serves the rest of the liturgy by illuminating meaning, and the liturgy as a whole surrounds the preaching with echoed imagery from the appointed texts in song and prayer. In the words of Origen, the sermon and the meal say the same thing: "bread (drink) of the word; bread (drink) of the eucharist."[10] The food of faith comes to the people in at least two ways.

Balancing Worship and Culture

It may be said that all churches today in some way base their worship on the word of God. Yet Scripture sets out numerous options, some of which even sit in conflict with each other. The truth is that *Scripture itself is based in worship*. The contents of the canon—the books that constitute the word of God—were chosen because of their importance to the people who gathered for worship. The writings that came to be most nourishing for the assembly formed the core of the writings that needed to be included in the canon. The earliest followers of Jesus gathered together after his death and heard the accounts of his appearances to various believers, and they continued to gather together in his name and to read the writing of the prophets and the apostles (remember Justin's description of worship). Gradually a body of literature grew that was dear to them in their meetings. They wanted to hear the stories again and again. The early churches, at least as recorded in certain documents, practiced their faith in many ways but fundamentally grounded worship in the writings they cherished. Those writings have become what we know as the Bible.

The word of God (which we have known for centuries as the canon of biblical Scripture) came out from the worship of the people. And the worship came out of the Holy Spirit's having gathered the people around the symbols of Christ's continuing presence in their midst. "Where two or three are gathered, there I am," Jesus had promised. But where the word is read, the word must also be interpreted.

Different days and times may call for different ways of worshiping. Sometimes a reading from Scripture and a sermon are called for. Sometimes silence is needed or prayer spoken or sung. After an alarming public tragedy, a prayer vigil is often needed where people gather in silence, in candlelight, for companionship and contemplation. There may be singing or a sermon and a meal. It is necessary for the worship leaders to know their communities and discern the most appropriate ways for God's presence among the people to be made clear.

When speaking this way about worship—that different times call for different worship—it can easily sound like worship is something the worship leaders create or dream up to suit the moment. That is not what is meant here. There is a pattern of trustworthy practices on which worship leaders draw in order to open the worship space to the people. These practices are handed on to each generation from the ancestors who gathered together in secret at first around the letters they had smuggled from one community to another, needing to hear the word of God because it strengthened them. They heard the apostle Paul writing to them, "I thank my God through Jesus Christ for all of you, because your faith is proclaimed throughout the world" (Rom. 1:8), and other empowering greetings.

We do not come together first and foremost to give something to God, but to lean on what God has already given to the church. Through the word, we hear God's voice. By eating bread, we taste God. In each other, as members of the body of Christ, we see God. We meet the Risen Christ in the assembly. We come to worship in various stages of faithfulness. Some of us may arrive with great spiritual confidence, rich with trust and direction. Others come with disabling questions, doubts, and fears. We cannot count on everyone feeling fervent in their convictions every Sunday. Many—perhaps most—of us come because we have not got the faith we desire. "Our hearts are restless, Lord, until they rest in thee," Augustine prayed.[11] We bring our restlessness to worship. And there we are met by the word that convicts and emboldens, the word that points the way and shows us images of the kingdom of God prepared for us. We hear about the present day and the end of time. We are given many tasks to do and the means to face them, fed by bread of word and bread of wheat.

At the same time, the actual event of worship will welcome many different rhythms, time frames, gestures, and "styles," all moving toward the same goal: the presence of God as promised among God's people. The richness and paradox of God's word invites every worshiping community to attend to how its worship reflects its culture. This can be a minefield of difficulty. What is of God? What is of the culture? How do we distinguish? If we are committed to a certain way of doing worship, is it because that is a gift of our ancestors, or is it a once worthy but now stultifying habit? Can a non-Native American culture grasp the use of sweetgrass smoke as incense? Can a non-Hispanic community be formed around a mariachi mass? Can a northern European culture sing South African freedom songs?

In order to think through these questions, the Lutheran World Federation convened an ecumenical group of liturgical theologians from all over the world. They met in Nairobi, Kenya, to examine the crucial and difficult balance between worship and culture/s. The product of their work is the 1996 publication, "The Nairobi Statement on Worship and Culture: Contemporary Challenges and Opportunities."[12] The document found that cultural practices and patterns are echoed in worship in four modes:

1. Worship practices are *transcultural*: "The resurrected Christ whom we worship, and through whom by the power of the Holy Spirit we know the grace of the Triune God, transcends and indeed is beyond all cultures."[13] A Christian worship experience is not entirely inculturated, according to Nairobi. While Jesus of Nazareth was born in Bethlehem and died in

Jerusalem, living in human history, we proclaim his resurrection as an event that gives hope in a transcendent reality to everyone despite cultural differences. For a balanced relationship between worship and culture, the transcultural will find expression in the whole liturgy, supporting the sermon's proclamation of universally applicable good news.

2. Worship practices are *contextual.* We know Christ because of the particularity in which he revealed himself to the world as a specific human born in a historical time and place. Jesus of Nazareth, we believe, was not an amorphous vapor but a fully human man who lived among us. The Risen Christ is revealed to the people of God through media particularized *in* culture: places of gathering differ, as do ways of greeting and moving together, songs, food, modes of offering, patterns of prayer. All of these and more are created out from a given community. The context is the means through which the Risen Christ becomes real to a people. If the context is completely ignored, if the local breads are not used for the meal, if the Scriptures are not proclaimed in the language of the people, if the songs have no relationship to the rhythms of the marketplace or festival celebrations of the nationality or race, Christ remains invisible. Because God created the world, because Jesus became incarnate in it, because the Holy Spirit moves among the people now, the context within which we live and move and have our being is blessed and can be relied upon as a necessary location for the revelation of the Lord.

Churches may bring into their sanctuaries plants of the local environment, bake bread made of local grains or rices, bring water from the local river or lake for the baptismal font, use artwork made by local potters, sculptors, painters, and quilters to tell the stories of God's work among us on earth. The dances of the people may be used to express community for a Sunday when such movement best connects to the word of God. Any means of using God's gifts to proclaim the gospel, from any cultural heartland, may be useful to the congregation. The test for faithful use of such gifts has to do with its grounding in God's word. The worship serves the word. Serving the word is local as well as universal.

3. Worship practices are *countercultural*. The word of God does not endorse all human desires, but rather opposes those forces that endanger, oppress, distort, and do harm. God's word in Romans 12:2 exhorts the people not to be conformed to this world but to be transformed. Some of the work of transformation requires preaching that corrects and admonishes, proclamation that intervenes in destructive life patterns, and opposes public policies that run counter to God's call to care for those in need. The prophetic word from the pulpit is supported by hymns of lament and stewardship, prayers that lift up the lowly, and a meal that feeds each person equally.

4. Worship practices are *cross-cultural*. This refers to the many ways a particular worshiping community can include in its worship reminders of cultures other than its own. To sing the songs of others reminds the assembly that the triune God is for all people everywhere. The texts, then, become the reason for the song, not familiarity alone or tradition or availability. It was not so many decades ago that the songs of the church were thought to be the province of particular denominations or cultural groups. That divisiveness has dissipated. We do not segregate the church's music but find that each body is enriched by the music of others. We strive to learn as many tunes and texts as possible. Today's Internet and printing capabilities make sharing music and other liturgical resources among churches very easy. Many churches that have experimented with different worship services on Sunday, defining them especially by different musical "styles," have now come to speak of "blended" worship in which many musical expressions are used in every service. In worship that strives to include cross-cultural elements, worshiping communities have a concrete way—through music—to break through racial, ethnic, and cultural barriers. Music is not the only vehicle for cross-cultural expression. On Pentecost in many churches, the story of the coming of the Holy Spirit in tongues of fire is read in several languages.

Worship that maintains a balance among these four ways in which worship relates to culture will have a strong plumb line for measuring liturgical choices. Consider the many elements in worship that speak to this balance. If a sermon and a song endorse wealth as a gift of faith (to use an extreme but not uncommon example), the liturgy endorses secular values and fails to critique the culture. The worship, then, remains predominantly *contextual* because it reflects and upholds a love for riches. Where, then, is the prophetic—the *countercultural*—voice? Shall the church be silent in the face of usury, of stealing from the poor, of dishonoring elders, or ignoring the needs of the blind and the lame? A countercultural word will build the identity of the Christian community as one that does not simply accept and endorse all of society's values.

Intercessory prayers that raise up the well-being of nations and racial groups other than the assembly's own keep worship *cross-cultural*. When an assembly sings outside its own cultural comfort zone, learning the music of strangers, the people are encouraged to know something about their sisters and brothers on the other side of the world. Where the worship service is all about the *contextual* issues of our neighborhood or nation and fails to mention God, there is, then, no *transcultural* element. Where, then, does the church differ from a popular and beneficial civic organization?

If worship leaders occasionally review the contents—especially Scripture readings, sermon content, prayers, and music—in order to notice the weight given to these four relations to culture, it will be possible to discern whether the worship for that particular assembly is balanced.

The word of God is complex, paradoxical, interpreted from any community's social location, including its cultural values and patterns. God's word—at the heart of the liturgy, whatever the shape (Holy Communion, ante-communion, or Praise and Worship)—is both reflective of culture and in tension with it. Worship that maintains an ancient structure and remains in a flexible and ambivalent relationship to the word of God has the best possibility of faithfully edifying the assembly.

Chapter 2

Serving a Pattern

When Justin wrote in 150 c.e. that the preacher "exhorts us into the pattern of these good things" (see chapter 1), what did he mean? What is this "pattern"? What are the "good things?" Is the use of the word *pattern* a different theology or less threatening than, for example, saying that the preacher exhorts the people to follow Jesus' "example"? Some translations of Justin's description of preaching say that the preacher "exhorts us to imitate" what is read. Such a reading of the use of Scripture would indicate that preaching primarily concerns itself with behavior, with reconfiguring of actions, rather than with transforming hearts. To be brought into a "pattern" is different. It is not about rules for life. It is about seeing in a new orientation.

Part of that pattern construction is dependent on reading the Scripture so the people can hear God's word clearly. We do not know from Justin exactly what Scriptures the people heard read or what was in the preacher's exhortation. We only know that the Scriptures were read. The place of word in worship is dramatically altered when there is no reading of Scripture. Where the scriptural text is only folded into the exhortation, the assembly has no opportunity to hear God's word as an uninterpreted voice. When Scripture is read aloud, offered to the assembly's ear—apart from the sermon—the people have an opportunity to listen to it before it is mediated through the preacher's understanding.

Because the preacher will illuminate the Scripture text(s) in her or his own way, the preaching can benefit by the Scripture being first read by someone else who has given thought to the meaning as well. Further, the

Scripture reading will yield more opportunity for the assembly to hear and receive the word of the Lord if it is done with care: practiced, confident, audible. The reading will—even in subtle ways with an emphasis here, a pause there—shed some light on the text. The assembly, then, receives first the reader's and then the preacher's interpretation with time to mull over its own understanding of the texts before the sermon addresses them. Over time, the assembly is enriched in its understanding of Scripture by hearing texts read by different persons. Especially when the congregation is small and people know each other outside of church, the biblical readings can come alive in surprising ways through interpretations that arise out of diverse personal histories. This plethora of opportunities to visit the texts, try them on, and ruminate, is part of the pattern into which God's word, read in worship, invites us. Faith is located between the texts, in the assembly's hearing disparate texts and working to fit them into a sensible shape. And then, with the readings set next to the sermon, a way of knowing is established that draws the assembly into a new reality.

How did this patterning begin?

Re-forming the Church

However much Protestants have differed from each other in the centuries since the Reformation, they began with a common critique of the liturgy as it was then practiced in the Western church, reacting against what they considered to be such excessive ceremony that the primary focus of worship was obscured. In fact, the word of God was smothered. Martin Luther's 1523 revision of the Sunday worship makes clear the evangelical commitment to word as well as sacrament rather than to what he considered to be nonsalvific, and therefore unnecessary, amendments to the liturgy. He did not throw away the worship in its entirety as he had experienced and led it, but he removed from it ceremonial actions that obscured the central, saving elements to draw more attention to what was most vital for faith.

> It is not now nor ever has been our intention to abolish the liturgical service of God completely, but rather to purify the one that is now in use from the wretched accretions which corrupt it and to point out an evangelical use. We cannot deny that the mass, i.e., the communion of bread and wine is a rite divinely instituted by Christ himself and that it was observed first by Christ and then by the apostles, quite simply and evangelically without any

additions. But in the course of time so many human inventions were added to it that nothing except the names of the mass and communion has come down to us.[1]

Accordingly, Luther laid out a simple order for worship, including some parts of the Roman rite he found unobjectionable but which could either be included or omitted. For the sake of clarity about what is meant by the Lutheran Reformers' terms, I have added in brackets the headings for the worship order that liturgical scholars have come in recent decades to embrace as the shape of the ecumenical ordo.[2]

[GATHERING]
    Introit (usually a chanted psalm of praise)
    Kyrie and Gloria (prayer for mercy and hymn of praise)
    Prayer (Collect, also called the Prayer of the Day)

[WORD]
    Epistle (read in the vernacular)
    Gradual (sung greeting the Gospel reading)
    Gospel (read in the vernacular)
    Creed
    Sermon

[MEAL] Mass (Holy Communion)
    Great Thanksgiving ("The Lord be with you. And also with you . . .")
    Preface (seasonal prayer that introduces giving thanks to God)
    Words of Institution ("On the night in which he was betrayed . . .")
    Lord's Prayer
    Lamb of God (hymn)
    Distribution of bread and wine

[SENDING]
    Benediction

Luther dismissed the idea that each piece and the order in which they appear are necessary. He even said of the sermon: "We do not think that it matters whether the sermon in the vernacular comes after the Creed or before the introit of the mass; although it might be argued that since the Gospel is the voice crying in the wilderness and calling unbelievers to faith, it seems particularly fitting to preach before mass."³ (Here, the word *mass* refers to the meal rather than the whole service.) Notice that Luther thought the sermon could begin the service or follow the profession of faith. Yet, while even the order of the worship was to some extent *adiaphora* in the Reformers' theology (meaning it would not "save" anyone because salvation is not achieved through the human expression of faith but only by God), Luther makes two important points about the relationship of the word to the meal.

First, because faith comes from hearing the gospel, and faith is needed in order to receive the meal, the word should be preached before the meal is eaten. Setting the word read and preached before the meal is a theological matter having to do with how the Holy Spirit's work is understood. The crucial question is, Do the people arrive at church on Sunday already full of faith or do they come to be renewed, to receive faith again and again, through the word of God? The question has been answered in divergent ways theologically and creates a particular divide between those communions that say the believer cannot summon faith but only can receive it and those that believe the receipt or assent to faith is owing to an inner holiness. What a liturgical event contains and how it is ordered depends upon how the church understands the people and how the church intends to reinforce the faith it means to express.

Second, for the sake of the people, Luther held that the liturgy should not change too drastically, for the reasons stated above: the people identify their faith with certain practices. To suddenly rip away those practices can damage faith. This, he held, is

> partly because of the weak in faith, who cannot suddenly exchange an old and accustomed order of worship for a new and unusual one, and more so because of the fickle and fastidious spirits who rush in like unclean swine without faith or reason, and who delight only in novelty and tire of it as quickly, when it has worn off. Such people are a nuisance even in other affairs, but in spiritual matters, they are absolutely unbearable.⁴

Although worship need not be conducted everywhere in the exact same way, Luther insisted that worship not be altered so that it harmed those of fragile faith. Writing of the charge following the sermon, Luther insisted that "We cannot have one do it one way today, and another, another way tomorrow, and let everybody parade his talents and confuse the people so that they can neither learn nor retain anything."[5] Calvin agreed, insisting that "in order to avoid all confusion, you must not allow that anyone by his insolence, and to put the congregation to derision, should come to disturb the order you have adopted."[6]

Most significantly for our purposes, the Reformers' order for worship required public reading of the Holy Scriptures—from both the Epistles and the Gospels—and especially in the language of the people. Only a few years after Martin Luther's revision of the Sunday liturgy, John Calvin's *Institutes* insisted as well that the word is central to the church's worship: "We must be apprised that faith has a perpetual relation to the word, and can no more be separated from it, than rays of light from the sun . . . to hear, generally means to believe."[7]

It is therefore no surprise that the mid-seventeenth-century West-minster *Directory for the Publique Worship of God* calls for the reading of "one Chapter of each Testament . . . at every meeting: and sometimes more, where the chapters be short, or the coherence of matter requireth it."[8] The readings were to be continuous—that is, portions of books would be read, and at each meeting, the reading was to begin where it left off the previous week. This continuity of reading Scripture readily allows for an especially didactic purpose to preaching, since the whole of a book over time can be studied and lectured on through the sermon.

Prayer followed the reading so that the assembly could be prepared to receive the saving word.[9] It was a prayer of confession and contrition so that those assembled may "be rightly affected with their Sinnes, that they may all mourn in sense thereof before the Lord, and hunger and thirst after the grace of God in Jesus Christ . . ."[10] Here again is an invitation to honesty that allows the word to penetrate. The sermon, following this confessional prayer, then, dealt with a theme from the Scripture reading. "Ordinarily, the subject of his Sermon is to be some Text of Scripture, holding forth some principle or head of Religion; or suitable to some speciall occasion emergent; or he may goe on in some Chapter, Psalme, or Booke of the holy Scripture as he shall see fit . . ."[11] Following the sermon, a prayer of thanksgiving was said by the preacher, a psalm might be sung, and then the assembly was dismissed. In short, the assembly gathered (solemnly), the minister prayed, read the Scriptures, prayed, preached, prayed, the assembly sang a psalm and was dismissed. Here is Gathering, Word, Response, Sending—what some churches now call a Service of the Word.

Even in the mid-nineteenth-century revival pattern, Gorham's *Camp Meeting Manual* delineates an entire complex of activities surrounding the preaching. Preaching was not expected to arise out of its own volition but needed to be nurtured and accompanied by the gathering, the preacher's family, and even the whole community. The preacher rose early and led family prayer at breakfast. Before the noon meal he held a prayer meeting and preached, preached twice in the afternoon followed by prayer each time, stopped for tea, preached at 7:30 P.M., and then held a prayer meeting until 10:00 P.M. It was a long day! Preaching and prayer, however, did not stand alone. "A very appropriate method of closing the services is, after taking the names of such as have been converted, with the view to proper future attentions to them, to administer the sacrament of the Lord's supper."[12] Even at the camp meeting, the meal of bread and wine instituted by Jesus closed the revival.

The Reformation's liturgical changes embraced what might be called a flexible stability: certain core treasures of worship define what happens on Sunday mornings *as* worship, and while their presence is necessary (both for the requisite "stability" and for the benefit of the people who have come to rely on them), the ways in which these treasures are included and conducted must enjoy some freedom by virtue of the Holy Spirit's movement in creative, surprising, and even disruptive ways.

Above all, a pattern of good things was established and protected, and this commitment to gathering the people around more than one text, more than one sign of God's grace, persists.

Finding Ecumenical Commonality

Several ecumenical endeavors uphold the centrality of word and sacrament. Following fifty years of consultations, conferences, and ecumenical dialogues, in 1983, the Faith and Order Commission of the World Council of Churches (WCC) published *Baptism, Eucharist, and Ministry* (*BEM*) affirming the commonality of liturgical practice through the centuries. "Most significantly, over a hundred churches from virtually every geographical area and ecclesiastical tradition returned detailed comments,"[13] including Protestants, Roman Catholics, and Orthodox churches.

Another Faith and Order Commission consultation in 1994 resulted in the document, "So We Believe, So We Pray: Towards Koinonia in Worship (The Ditchingham Letter and Report)."[14] It brought together thirty-two representatives from many denominations.[15] While it does not enjoy the imprimatur of having official WCC adoption (as does *BEM*), it is an insightful statement from a diverse group of liturgical theologians and constitutes yet another step on the way toward fuller understanding between Christian churches. In addition, the work of these consultations moves the churches closer toward being able to share in full communion.[16]

Relevant to our concerns, the Ditchingham document, as it is sometimes called, looks toward further ecumenical unity: "Besides the work already done on baptism, eucharist and ministry, the churches need to address the renewal of preaching, the recovery of the meaning of Sunday and the search for a common celebration of *Pascha* [holy week] as *ecumenical theological concerns*."[17] Note the attention to a renewal of preaching in relation to broader concerns for the worship life of the church.

In the section on inculturation of worship (the adaptation of worship practices to include particular local expressions) the consultation laid out some "basic principles emerging from the nature of Christian worship." Among them is the principle that worship is "biblically grounded; hence the Bible is one indispensable source of worship's language, signs, and prayers . . ."[18] God's word is central in shaping all the other elements of worship because worship is "a privileged occasion at which God is present in the proclaimed Word, in the sacraments, and in the other forms of Christian prayer, as well as in the assembly gathered in worship . . ."[19] In a statement of liturgical criteria vital to the ecumenical shape of the liturgy, the consultation affirmed the following:

The usual liturgical components of the eucharist are: the reading and preaching of the word; intercession for the whole Church and the world; and, in accord with the actions of our Lord at the Last Supper, taking bread and wine to be used by God in the celebration; blessing God for creation and redemption; breaking the bread; and giving the bread and the wine. Tradition includes the recitation of the words of institution and the invocation of the Holy Spirit at the eucharistic prayer, and the recitation of the Lord's prayer.[20]

Here is the visible pattern of good things. In very real ways this contemporary delineation of the core of Christian worship accords with the depiction of worship among early Christians, allowing us to peer into our own practices and see in our patterns of movement and focus the gifts we have received and maintained from our ancestors.

It is perhaps easiest for most people to see the commonalities among the so-called liturgical churches.[21] Such worship services often appear to visitors as primarily rote, calm, formal, and unbending. They may also appear to be mysterious because the formality can give the impression of a stiffness that seems to enact a godliness unavailable to anyone who is not schooled in the secrets. But, in actuality, any worship service can appear mysterious and unapproachable to someone unfamiliar with the unwritten and unspoken rules of that particular assembly. As a result, newcomers may feel alienated because the service is conducted in an over-arching pattern that is much the same from week to week. Those who attend regularly understand the flow of the parts. Every liturgy can be inviting or uninviting, appear rote or spontaneous, calm or frenetic, formal or informal, manipulative or freeing, depending on the way it is conducted and the level of analysis being brought to bear on the experience.

Beyond the issues of the emotional climate created by the worship as a whole, a liturgical difference exists between denominations based in the aim or purpose of worship. This is a theological and not a merely stylistic issue. For the so-called liturgical churches, the pattern of worship is built on paradoxical symbols that intend to express the primacy of God's action in gathering the people for the nurturance of faith. These communions hold to the ancient traditions found in even the meager descriptions of early church worship from the *Didache* and Justin Martyr. They expect that God will be present where the word and the sacraments are offered, that faith needs to be renewed every Sunday, that the assembly meets to pray for the needs of the whole world and to be sent out at the end for the sake of the life of the world. The fact that worship preceded biblical canon means for them that the worship itself is primary theology (*prima theologia*)—that what the assembly *does* in worship every week *is* its theological statement.

The liturgical pattern in so-called nonliturgical churches—hearkening to Calvin or Zwingli or other Reformers in or since the sixteenth century— encompasses churches that have very clear worship patterns while leaving, in some cases, more room for innovation and spontaneity. Calling a nonliturgical church "free" refers especially to its ecclesiology: the level of congregational control over the church's decisions. A "free" church may or may not have a regularly called pastor. Members of the congregation may take turns leading worship and preaching or the church may be very hierarchical in its leadership. While the impression might be that there is no "liturgy," there could be no worship without gathering, and it would be rare to find a "free" church—or any church—that does not read Scripture, hear a sermon, sing, and pray. Nonliturgical churches share a worship pattern which they utilize in common with other "free" churches and with churches that do not hold a weekly communion meal (like the Service of the Word of so-called liturgical churches).

While Protestants might hold weekly Holy Communion worship or a Word Service and Roman Catholics observe the mass (Holy Communion), it is possible, although difficult, to speak of commonalities or of an ecumenical ordo. It is further complicated by the fact that, despite the range of worship patterns among Protestants, we can see even greater differences between Protestants and Orthodox. One of the editors of the *Ditchingham Report*, Dagmar Heller, has written elsewhere:

> Protestant churches generally allow the possibility for orders of worship to be freely created, while Orthodox worship, for example, stays with traditional forms. Worship is centered on the mystery of God and serves to unite human beings with God. Thus it has a deeply mystical component. Further, for the Orthodox, in contrast to Protestantism, the centre of a worship service is the Divine Liturgy, that is, the celebration of the eucharist, which cannot be shared with separated churches. Protestants regard a service of the word as a complete and fully valid worship service.[22]

For the Orthodox, the center is the meal, enacted through a liturgical expression believed to image the worship taking place in heaven throughout eternity. For Protestants, the center has been primarily in the word. In contrast, the ecumenical ordo reclaims a balance between word and meal—neither the Divine Liturgy of the Orthodox Church nor the Word Service of the Protestants but a bridge between both extremes. Ecumenical work like that done by the Faith and Order Commission speaks of an undergirding structure "which is to be perceived in the ordering and scheduling of the most primary elements of Christian worship. This 'ordo' . . . roots in word and sacrament held together."[23]

Renewing Time: The Church Calendar

The balance of word and sacrament constitutes one level of liturgical pattern that serves the word. Another level is time itself. For churches that follow a liturgical calendar, the year begins in December, about four weeks before Christmas, with the season of Advent. Thus, time itself begins even before the birth of the One who changes all time, and the calendar's acknowledgment of this eschatological event sets up the church to be a people whose lives run according to a clock apart from the norm. Because Advent is tied to the nativity of Jesus of Nazareth by leading into the celebration of his birth, it runs slightly counter to the secular Julian calendar that begins on January 1. The church calendar does not mark earthly seasons or academic schedules or the fiscal year. It follows the events and concerns of the church. The first half of the church calendar is focused on Jesus: his birth (Advent and Christmas), his baptism (Epiphany), the journey to his death (Lent), his crucifixion (Holy Week), resurrection (Easter), and the sending of the Holy Spirit (Pentecost Day). Following Pentecost, the calendar is trained on Scripture texts that instruct the church on being the body of Christ in the world. This is the Season after Pentecost which runs basically from spring through autumn, beginning with the feast of Holy Trinity and ending with Christ the King. These days are important in their own right because they are not tied to any events in the life of Jesus or of the churches but focus on doctrinal formulations about the identities of the triune God and the Christ. By following the church calendar and allowing it to determine the texts read and preached on a given Sunday, the congregation enters every year into the life of Christ and its own life in Christ. Thus, we are given another good pattern in which and by which to understand who we are as the body of Christ.

The liturgical calendar serves the preaching by reminding the preacher that a cycle of attentiveness is spiraling through the sermon's foci, every year bringing the congregation back to similar themes and images but always with a new twist because life has changed, national boundaries have been redrawn, different people are richer or poorer, new laws have been passed or not attended to, babies have been born and people have died. The world has changed. The sermon points to the unending steadfastness of the Lord through all the insecurity and uncertainty of human life as the texts keep returning and we hear them anew each time.

Receiving the Texts: Lectionaries

Lectionaries of readings evolved over centuries, and what we have today is a distillation of negotiated texts. They come from the readings that the church needed and wanted to hear as it developed its liturgical calendar, which year after year commemorates and celebrates the life of Jesus and the life of the church.

Following the Second Vatican Council, two ecumenical bodies formed to rework the ancient Roman lectionary that described the liturgical calendar: (1) the North American Consultation on Common Texts (CCT) made up of Catholic and Protestant liturgical scholars and (2) the International English Language Liturgical Consultation (ELLC).[24] Today CCT includes representatives from over twenty-five Protestant denominations as well as the Roman Catholic International Commission on English in the Liturgy (ICEL). CCT produced a lectionary in 1983 that was tested and revised for publication as the *Revised Common Lectionary* (RCL) in 1992.

The RCL is divided into three-year cycles (Years A, B, and C) based in the original Roman scheme. The Gospel readings for Year A come primarily from Matthew; Year B from Mark; and Year C, Luke. Texts from John are read each year for the festival days, so that much of John is heard every year while each of the other Gospels has its own year almost exclusively. Through the lenses of the different Gospels, the church enters into at least four ways of seeing Christ and the body of Christ, the church.

Three readings are assigned for each Sunday: (1) from the Old Testament or, during Easter, from Acts; (2) from the New Testament (a text from one of the Epistles, Acts, or Revelation); and (3) a Gospel text. As Walter Brueggemann[25] has insisted, the Old Testament text is essential particularly for its ability to help the church understand itself as a corporate body. Were the church to hear only the Gospel texts—or only the New Testament—there might be a tendency to take on an unbalanced picture of the life of faith as if it were simply an individualistic enterprise rather than being fed by the community. The Old Testament stories remind us of a *people* who experienced together and in diverse ways the power of God. For the assembly hearing three texts each Sunday, the word of God comes to life in counterpoint. The different images and themes interpret each other, driving the preaching to deeper levels because the preacher has to dig deep in order to reconcile the ideas.

The epistle text describes the church's struggles to interpret and appropriate the teachings and revelations of God's word. Through the epistle, the assembly is reminded of its ancestors in faith, the complexity of their wonderings about what they had seen and heard, their failings to embody what they believed, the repeated turning back and beginning again. The epistles give the church hope and also direction. They take the images and mystery from Old Testament stories of the community and Gospel stories of Jesus and his followers and turn them into something recognizably mirroring our own selves.

Finally, the Gospel is read. In the Reformers' understanding of how people come to faith, they emphasized God's power beyond all human effect: "God cannot be dealt with and cannot be grasped in any other way than through the Word."[26] And the gospel is preached. In "The Large Catechism," Martin Luther wrote that "Neither you nor I could ever know anything about Christ, or believe in him and receive him as Lord, unless . . . through the preaching of the gospel by the Holy Spirit. . . . [W]here Christ is not preached, there is no Holy Spirit to create, call, and gather the Christian church, apart from which no one can come to the Lord Christ."[27] Preaching serves the liturgy by letting the Holy Spirit make saints.

The Scripture texts for a given Sunday or sermon may come from this ecumenical lectionary formed by the church's liturgical calendar or the preacher will choose the text(s). In either practice, the Holy Spirit is at work through the Scripture texts read and preached. The Holy Spirit is at work through the church and through preachers, bringing together the word of God and the church's life. For churches whose preacher is responsible from week to week for the text selection, the Spirit will be working through the lives of the congregation members, the events of the community and the larger world, the preacher's prayer, and the preacher's insight into the congregation's needs, all to urge her or him toward the appropriate text(s) for that day.

While this lectionary does not purport to be a perfect answer to every problem with lectionaries (some stories are omitted, the continuity of biblical books is lost in piecemeal readings, and so forth), it does offer a wide range of texts, a wealth of imagery, a means by which assemblies and especially preachers can be ensured of hearing a healthy representation of God's word (not simply the preacher's favorite texts), and an avenue for ecumenical liturgical life. Preachers of diverse churches can work together in text study. Assemblies across denominations can share in the liturgical emphasis Sunday after Sunday. Use of the RCL relieves preachers of the temptation to focus repeatedly on subjects and texts that are amenable to them, rather than being challenged by difficult or unfamiliar biblical passages.

The Revised Common Lectionary is integrally tied to the liturgical calendar by

1. giving the congregation repeated opportunities to ponder familiar texts in a new light.
2. offering overarching thematic content to the sermon by situating the sermon each week in a larger observance of Jesus' witness and the church's life.
3. connecting worship, and the sermon in particular, to time itself.

The RCL bears witness to an observance of time that allows for a disjunction and disruption in the church's very understanding of time by being at odds with the secular calendar. The RCL creates, for example, a time for practicing patience and eschatological visioning in the weeks before Christmas—the Advent season—right when the secular world is holding parties, putting up joyous lights, and singing about the Savior having already arrived (along with Santa, of course). Advent does not invite the raucous joviality of the Christmas season, so for those who keep Advent (refraining from singing or hearing the carols, waiting to party until the actual Christmas season arrives, holding their emotional and spiritual lives in a kind of patience in the midst of frenzy), there is built into our lives a time of year when our disconnection from the secular world is stark. Advent is not a pensive time nor a penitent time as is Lent, but it is a time of being set apart from the norm. Every season can do this in its own way.

Preachers who find the lectionary a burden sometimes speak of having nothing new to say since the same texts are offered for preaching every three years. Of course, even those congregations that follow the liturgical calendar and use a lectionary (whether the RCL or another) are not required to follow it every Sunday. There may be times when, for pastoral reasons, another text is more apt. Indeed, while every congregation may well make its own decisions about the word read and preached on any given Sunday depending on its context, it is the expressed expectation that when the RCL is used, it gives visible unity to the church on earth and makes possible a shared communion in the word.[28] A liturgy guided by the RCL serves the preaching by offering the wisdom of the church in appointing texts that come out of an ancient memory, a pattern of faith.

Chapter 3

Ash Wednesday
A Case Study

In order to make concrete the process of preparing the sermon and the worship structure so that each nourishes the other and together they serve the word, this study will use an Ash Wednesday sermon I preached based on the RCL texts that appear on that day every year.

In figure 3.1, I lay out the primary focus of each reading with regard to human life and God's work in human concerns in order to compare them. We will first focus on exploring these texts and, then, in the following chapters, we will consider how these lections inform the whole liturgy— the options for prayer language, hymnody, shape of the space, and so on—that allow the rest of the liturgy to serve the preached word just as the preaching serves the liturgy as a whole.

READING	TEXT	HUMAN SITUATION	GOD'S ATTRIBUTES
First	Joel 2:1-2, 12-17	Responding to God's grace, we are called to blow the trumpet, rend our hearts, return to the Lord, fast, gather the people, weep	God is gracious and merciful, slow to anger, abounding in steadfast love
Epistle	2 Corinthians 5:20b—6:10	We live in the paradox of having nothing, yet possessing everything—in the paradox is reconciliation	NOW is the time when God's righteousness is made our salvation
Gospel	Matthew 6:1-6, 16-21	We need to give alms, pray, and fast in order to locate our treasure . . .	. . . when, all the while, the treasure is Christ Jesus, the heart of all life

Figure 3.1

The Texts

Because the Gospel reading is the linchpin of the lectionary texts, the Matthew reading is important to scrutinize first. It is particularly crucial to do a thorough job of analysis because the danger of hearing the same texts on a certain day every year is, of course, that they become familiar enough to make us believe we know what they are about. Beware! In addition, the clarity of this text's structure—broken into three parts that deal with the Lenten disciplines of almsgiving, prayer, and fasting—may tempt the preacher to a little laziness. This is not a text that gives the preacher license simply to remind the assembly that Lent is about giving up money (alms), time (prayer), and comfort (fasting). There is nothing to be gained by waving in front of the assembly a list of demands, as if that is what faith is all about.

Likewise, nothing is added to the faith of the assembly if the preacher focuses on the inherent us-vs.-them language of the text: "You should not be like *those hypocrites.*" In this text are myriad images of what we should not do during Lent: "do not sound a trumpet before you . . . do not be like the hypocrites . . . do not look dismal . . ." The underlying message of the good news during Lent has as its trajectory the cross and the resurrection at the end of Holy Week. Every text of the Lenten Sundays is rushing toward Gethsemane whose vision is one of salvation for all people. This gracious promise militates against dividing people into groups for the usefulness of the image. The truth is, we are all hypocrites, and the text is not simply a window but a mirror.

Instead of causing rancor among different kinds of people based on their piety, Ash Wednesday is meant to bring all people to the bottom of the dry well, to the place of nothingness, to the absence of pride and greed, to awareness of how much we fear not having enough, and to our distance from others' problems. Ash Wednesday takes us to our broken hearts and there offers us the treasure of true abundance.

The Old Testament reading from Joel is utterly focused on the heart. The prophet echoes the call for fasting, but rather than admonishing the assembly to certain ways of acting out the disciplines appropriate to faith, he takes it deeper: "Rend your hearts and not your clothing." The preacher may be tempted to land on the image of our fear over the "day of the LORD . . . a day of darkness and gloom . . ." by locating this coming fright on Golgotha since Ash Wednesday begins a period that ends at the Last Supper on Maundy Thursday. Clearly, Lent leads right to Jesus' death. Yet Joel is not concerned with death but with return to the real treasure because, facing devastation (which might take any number of forms), the only sure defense is in the Lord.

The preacher might ask of the epistle, What is this reading telling us about our own church? The epistle reading is best considered a picture of the church's task in the face of the truths shown in God's word: the situation of human life and God's actions in the world. Given the human need for almsgiving, prayer, and fasting, and God's promise of steadfast love (our treasure and heart), the epistle lays bare the church's direction. In 2 Corinthians 5, we see that the church is the image of hope: fear overturned, death engendering life.

Locating the *Hertzpunkt*

Preachers approach the lections in several ways. Some may choose one reading on which to preach; others, two lections. Still others (and this is my path—offered for those who might wish to try it) work on articulating the relationships among all three readings, especially based in that between the Old Testament and the Gospel readings, I look for what Martin Luther called the *hertzpunkt* ("heart point") in each lection and then search for what lies beneath it, binding all three lections.

On this particular Ash Wednesday—because of the socioeconomic climate, political realities, local concerns, the assembly's current issues—I heard the relationship between the Old Testament and the Gospel lections as an integral connection that exists between (1) turning toward the Lord in disciplines that express the relationship we have with God, and (2) realizing God's graciousness through disciplines that reach out toward others. Through fasting, we know the hunger of others; through almsgiving, we see the suffering in our midst; through prayer, the needs of the world become our own. The disciplines reveal one's own heart, one's own treasure.

While another preacher might find the *hertzpunkt* of the epistle and Gospel lections (or Old Testament and epistle) to be the most compelling, I find a congruence of theme in all three lections and then splay that open through one prime image or one lection.[1] In the end, the assembly may think the sermon deals with only one text while, in reality, the preacher is simply using one text to preach about the underlying message of them all.

Preachers may contend that all three texts do not mesh on a Sunday, especially when the lectionary uses semi-continuous readings. I contend that if you look deeply enough into each text for the rendering of the human situation (What are we up against? Where are our faults? What is our struggle?) and of the steadfastness of God (Where is God acting in this text? How is God's presence and promise changing the situation? What in our own situation is an analogous place to locate God's work in the world?), and you boil that into a single sentence, a profound commonality between texts emerges. The advantage of being forced to dive more deeply into all three texts in order to find the basis of their commonality, the *hertzpunkt*, is that it does not let the preacher settle too quickly on what seems to be the obvious "message" of the texts. For, in fact, the lections are not merely holding up for us a life-fixing manual but inviting us into a mystery. To reach toward the *hertzpunkt* is to grapple with the truth that cannot be named in only one way but always needs at least two faces. In addition to the texts working together to speak both reality (human situation) and hope (God's activities) into the present time, the Sunday's place in the church year undergirds the texts with thematic depth.

Ash Wednesday is the day on which the assembly hears the words, "Remember that you are dust and to dust you shall return." Churches that do not hold strictly to the liturgical calendar nevertheless often observe Ash Wednesday and Lent or at least the Lenten season leading up to the resurrection at Easter. The movement through Lenten Sundays raises images of a comprehensive description of the life of faith. Despite the fact that Ash Wednesday every year calls for the same texts, in each of Years A, B, and C a thematic thread is visible moving outward from the Ash Wednesday focus.

In the following schema in figure 3.2, I use the Lenten texts for Year C simply to demonstrate the continuity they have with Ash Wednesday.[2]

SUNDAYS IN LENT, YEAR C	GOSPEL TEXT	CONTENTS	THEME
First	Luke 4:1-13	Jesus is tempted in the wilderness	Difficulty in life
Second	Luke 13:31-35	Jesus weeps over Jerusalem	Sorrow
Third	Luke 13:1-9	John cries repentance; the man pleads for the fig tree	Metanoia
Fourth	Luke 15:1-3, 11b-32	Parable of the prodigal son and merciful father	Forgiveness
Fifth	John 12:1-8	Mary anoints Jesus' feet; Judas objects	Gratitude

Figure 3.2

If we think about the heart of these lections as a mirror for our own lives as persons belonging to the body of Christ, we can see a movement from Jesus' baptism (and our baptisms) toward a temptation to turn away from that gift. Following the joy and beauty of baptism, we come up out of the water, look around, and notice that the world seems unconcerned about the vision we hold. In response to this world so disconnected from those things Jesus proclaimed in the desert, we hear a cry for repentance. What else can a people do who live in such a materialistic, power-hungry, proof-thirsty world as the one Jesus faced in the wilderness, the one we inhabit in all ages? "Repent!" cries the Baptist. "Please give it one more chance!" cries the gardener on the Third Sunday in Lent. Then we hear of the prodigal (who is each of us), the elder son (who is also each of us), and the father (who is not us) but who runs to embrace and celebrate the wayward son. This story raises up all of our fears about earning God's love. We believe that, at some level, obedience is demanded of us and if we do not adhere to the rules, we should ask for the punishment we deserve. The gracious surprise is that the father does not punish. He only rejoices, calling for gifts and honors to be bestowed on his child. And when the elder complains about his brother's special treatment, the father gives him, as well, undying love: "All that is mine is yours." We cannot fathom this generosity. At last, just before Holy Week begins with Jesus' procession into the heart of power riding on a donkey, honored as a savior, and then crucified, we hear the story of Mary defying the values of the worldly-wise—those like Judas—in order to truly honor the one whose life gave her new life.

Each of the stories in these texts is rich with characters whose roles invite all kinds of new melodies, images, theological conundrums written in large and subtle ways, and minor points that could become major aids toward the congregation's deepened faith. The primary themes can be described in diverse terms. The main issue is to see that a structure exists in these readings, a structure that takes the congregation deeper and deeper into the fundamental experience of Lent: the contemplation of the crucifixion and resurrection that governs our reckoning of time. Everything flows out from Sunday, and all Sundays flow out from the Resurrection of Our Lord on Easter Sunday.

The sermon, then, has as a part of its task to reorient the assembly into the teachings of the liturgical year. The sermon will, in part, set the lections in the context of the whole calendar, telling the assembly of the value of the season at hand, how the church moved from the previous time to the present, and into what the season leads. It may not do so in explicit terms but will have this goal in mind. In this way, through the calendar, the liturgy serves the preaching, and the preaching opens up the significance of time.

In the following chapters, we will look at how the Emmaus story guides the preparation of the Sunday worship, and we will consider the various aspects of the liturgy so that, based in God's word, they each serve the preaching.

Sermon for Case Study[3]

The worship service took place at the Lutheran Theological Seminary at Philadelphia. The assembly included seminarians, faculty, staff, visitors, and local judicatory officials from the various denominations that the students represent. The seminary sanctuary is a white square room with timbered ceiling, light, and stained-glass windows. Pews have been replaced with chairs set in choir pattern facing each other four rows deep on each side. The aisle separating the chairs has at one end the pulpit and font; at the other, the table.

Ash Wednesday

Texts: Joel 2:1-2, 12-17; 2 Corinthians 5:20b—6:10; Matthew 6:1-6, 16-21
Melinda Quivik—Lutheran Theological Seminary at Philadelphia
25 February 2009[4]

The church wants us to hear these same words every single year:
Blow the trumpet! The day of darkness is almost here! Gather everybody together!—
Everybody!—Old and young. Even infants. Call a fast.
Rend your hearts . . . not your clothing. Now is the time!
Treasures on earth will not bless you. If you are looking for admiration from other people, forget it. *Give alms! Pray! Fast!* Do these things in secret.
Turn toward the One Holy God who covets your well-being.

Having nothing, you possess everything.
Your Father in heaven, who created you and knew you before you were born, will know.
That is all that matters.

Having nothing, you possess everything.

Every single year we hear this. Every single year we need to hear it again.
We don't believe it.

> What d'ya mean, it doesn't matter what other people think of me . . . ?!
>> My candidacy committee wants me to see a therapist.
>> They're scrutinizing my every move.
>> My colleagues are judging me all the time—
>>> whether I'm teaching well, publishing enough, doing enough good works.
>> My congregation is frustrated because we can't sing carols during Advent, and now we can't say the A-word [Alleluia] during Lent.

We buried the A-word on Transfiguration Sunday in many of our churches.

It's a reminder of the power of words to form us . . . and to disfigure us.
> Some people call such liturgical practices a kind of tyranny.
> Those liturgists, you know . . . telling us what to do.
>> As if it didn't matter what we do when God calls us to gather together!
>> As if what happens in worship is not worthy of our most exacting scrutiny.

The burial of a word for a time is no small thing.
It is wisdom . . . because words matter.

The prophet Joel cries out:
Rend your hearts . . . not your clothing.
Break your treasure, in other words. Not something inconsequential.
BREAK your TREASURE! Not even just something you love . . . but the very core of you: your HEART. Tear it open. Crush it.

What do you hold onto the most tightly right now? What do you cling to?
What seems most essential this year, right now? Ambition? Success? Getting your way?
Coming out on top? Being admired? Conforming? Not making waves? Disturbing others by making a point? All of the above?

The church today wants us to hear these words: *Rend your hearts . . . not your clothing.*
Remember you are dust and to dust you will return . . . because . . .
when we hear we are dust, we can be sure we are hearing the truth.
There is no mincing of words in this. There is no hiding anywhere.
Wherever we go, we are dust . . . and, in the end, ashes.

Clothing has nothing to do with who we are.
The outer trappings have nothing to do with whose we are.
Having nothing, we possess everything.
Crushed, broken, contrite at the center of our lives IS where Lenten ashes lead us.

Last summer in Montana, I saw miles of ashes. I peered at them. I laid down in them.
I went hunting morel mushrooms with two friends who know where to look.
We went to Wise River . . . a beautiful valley ringed by timber-rich mountains.
We stopped at the Forest Service to get a map of the most recent burns . . . places where fires had swept through the summer before. It had been a hot summer—not as devastating as Australia has been lately—but just as severe.

You know—when you are driving through the mountains, especially on narrow two-lane roads or one-track gravel roads, you can't see the landscape for the trees.
You can't see the forest for the trees!
So it was very eerie to be riding along, looking through hillsides of blackened tree trunks left standing with no branches or needles, no bushes beneath them, the contours of the forest floor utterly visible, cleared of all obstruction. No green . . . no shade. Painful.

We pulled over and walked on the black earth . . . went our separate ways to comb the ground . . . wearing our worst shoes because they'd be impossible to clean.

(If you hunt morels a lot, you have morel-hunting shoes, pants, and
sweatshirt.)

You walk slowly, crunching chunks of burned twigs and bark underfoot.
You hear no birds. No squirrels or rabbits. They can't stand to be there.
There is no food for them. Everything is ash.
You look at the base of trees for a little brown Christmas-tree-shaped
mushroom
whose sides are like brain tissue—fissures and ridges.
(They are really, really tasty, even though they look like brains.)
You want to find a little place where there's just enough moisture, sun,
and shade . . . underneath a fallen log . . . beneath a big root . . . And
there will be one or two—or a little forest of—Christmas tree morels.
You squeal and pluck them into your bucket.

> Morels are so expensive that in previous summers there were knife
> fights in the mountains. Interlopers from other states had come to
> take the mushrooms back to market. A law was finally passed that
> every Montanan is allowed five pounds of morels for their own
> consumption every summer. Interlopers have to pay.
>
> (Sometimes you can get that much! Dry them and eat all year.)

As I squinted for the prize
here and there
in the devastated landscape
I saw a tiny blade of grass
coming right up through several inches of thick ashes . . . as if the ash was
fine black soil.
Not many blades of grass, mind you. But ashes release nutrients that
wouldn't otherwise be there in such abundance.

Nitrogen feeds grasses. Fire breaks open softwood tree cones and seeds.
New life comes forth. Hidden deep beneath the ashy forest floor are
the seeds of something new.
Dust to dust . . . ashes to ashes.

You and I are dust and ashes. Something new is being born in you and in
me today.

Something new—or so old it has been long forgotten—comes to us when
   our hearts are crushed and our spirits dried to dust and ashes.
We don't know where it will appear . . . under what log or rock outcrop-
   ping . . .
what it will look like.
It may be very tiny, even invisible. It may grow slowly.
Yet, when it seems as if there is nothing there . . . when you possess nothing . . . when your heart has been broken . . . your landscape stripped
   bare . . . THEN is when God sees the one thing God wants:

   The sacrifice acceptable to God is a troubled [broken, humble] spirit;
   a troubled and broken [contrite, crushed] heart, O God, you will not
   despise. (Ps. 51:17)

In the ashes, in our greatest need, in a time of horrendous trial or even
a momentary disappointment, there in the dust lies our hope. *There* is
where the One who died and rose
has already been . . . and always waits for us.
   + + +

Chapter 4

Gathering

The disciples were walking together and talking.

Now on that same day two of them were going to a village called Emmaus, about seven miles from Jerusalem, and talking with each other about all these things that had happened. While they were talking and discussing, Jesus himself came near and went with them, but their eyes were kept from recognizing him. And he said to them, "What are you discussing with each other while you walk along?" They stood still, looking sad. Then one of them, whose name was Cleopas, answered him, "Are you the only stranger in Jerusalem who does not know the things that have taken place there in these days?" He asked them, "What things?" They replied, "The things about Jesus of Nazareth, who was a prophet mighty in deed and word before God and all the people, and how our chief priests and leaders handed him over to be condemned to death and crucified him. But we had hoped that he was the one to redeem Israel. Yes, and besides all this, it is now the third day since these things took place. Moreover, some women of our group astounded us. They were at the tomb early this morning, and when they did not find his body there, they came back and told us that they had indeed seen a vision of angels who said that he was alive. Some of those who were with us went to the tomb and found it just as the women had said; but they did not see him." (Luke 24:13-24)

According to the Emmaus story, the two disciples are walking together, deep in conversation about the women who, just that day, had found Jesus' tomb empty. The women told the other disciples about this strange turn of events, and so it makes sense that the two walking on the road to Emmaus would be huddled together and dismayed—they are grieving! They had lost their teacher.

We know they are consumed with grief and confusion because the story tells us that when Jesus—the stranger they did not recognize—joins them, he asks what has happened that so engages them. They tell of their hopes for Jesus' leadership and that, while struggling to grasp his death and burial, they suddenly had to contend with the disturbing truth that the body was gone.

The questioning that has consumed these two gives the stranger on the road an opening to explain to them a new way of seeing what has happened. He invites them to interpret the events in light of what has already been revealed to them in God's word. The two disciples are together because of the experience they have had in common—first, as followers of Jesus of Nazareth and now, as fellow mourners, puzzled by their next steps, aghast at what they have heard from the women.

They are together because of Jesus, the one we speak of today as the Word of God. He is the one who has brought them together. His word is the heart of what still brings his followers together. But it is not only Jesus as Word of God who gathers the people; something about that Word, some eternal mystery, some compelling hope, calls us to walk the road toward a place of refuge where we join with others.

Gathering Begins with Need

If the situation of the two disciples walking to Emmaus indicates to us something about our own gathering, we notice, among other things, that the meeting of these two is grounded in their need. They are in mourning, confounded.

There is plenty in our world over which we may grieve—if only for the sake of someone else—even in the midst of joy. When it is not ourselves or our immediate neighbors who are enduring hard times, it is someone else's neighbor. When we look at God's word—as witnessed by the depiction of truth telling on the road to Emmaus—we see the necessity for honesty, for opening wounds, for real lament, for speaking sorrow and fear. When we are aware of our connectedness to others, our common ultimate help-lessness regarding the alleviation of suffering and the tenuousness of our own good fortune, we do, in fact, gather together as beggars. God's word pulls us toward each other where we are then fed by the many ways in which God's presence manifests the resurrection mystery. It is not *we* who gather ourselves, but *God* who gathers us. The impetus that compels us to walk the road with friends—and there be accompanied by a wisdom that opens the word even more fully—is God's, not ours.

God's Word Engages the Assembly

How does the Gathering serve the preaching? When we gather, we are brought into contact with other creatures who, like ourselves, are created in the image of God. Anything can happen! We might be invited to try out an insight that could never have come to our consciousness alone in our own living rooms or on the street! The gathering itself promises new vision and remarkable transformations that could not be anticipated in isolation. Greeting, singing, and praying—the beginning of the liturgy—serve the preaching by introducing the assembly to its gathering at a particular time in the church calendar[1] and to the themes of the texts. This is why a worship service cannot be the same thing experienced "virtually" as it is experienced in person. There is, in fact, nothing "virtual" about God's presence in our lives. It is not "almost" but "absolutely." It is not merely an idea but an existential reality.

While God's word brings people together, that gathering begins even before the people actually assemble, just as the two disciples walked along the road together to meet the others at Emmaus. Immediately after each Sunday assembly, the people start to prepare for the next one. Some will organize or practice some aspect of the coming worship: prepare the music, rehearse with the choir, sing new music, learn more about leading the congregation's song. Sometimes the participation has to do with preparing the worship space—cleaning, rearranging, repairing, decorating. The preparation may be praying for the needs of the world, for congregations everywhere, for preachers and presiders, and for people who need prayer. Where a lectionary is used, the preparation involves deep immersion in the Scripture texts for the coming Sunday so that, in addition to the preacher, the assembly arrives with knowledge of the themes and images that the worship might encompass.

The Gathering involves everyone at some level in some ways. The preparation begins at home the week before with prayer, reading, and studying the coming Scripture texts. A calendar of the readings for the year might be made available in print or online to help the people look ahead. A brief temple talk after worship during the announcements could encourage the people to read and ponder the texts for the next week.

We might think of the daily and weekly preparations for Sunday being a dance. As the people of God, we move about in our separate and inter-connected realms of work and play. We find ourselves bearing the witness of the Sunday worship into every aspect of our weekday lives as if we are each carrying bread to the hungry and drink to the thirsty. We do not always fulfill our own best hopes for what that offering might produce, and we probably forget that we ourselves are, in fact, bread and wine to be broken and poured out for the well-being of others. But if we can imagine and hold in mind the connection between Sunday and every other day of ourselves as bread for the world, the power of God's word will reveal itself in unimaginable ways in every one of our vocations. The disciples who fled to Emmaus had no expectation that they would encounter something unbelievable. We who live in God's word expectantly look each day for signs of God's work in the world. Daily we walk *from* the word *toward* the word. We gather because the word gives unbelievable visions of a realm in which all creatures, lands, and people are honored, nurtured, and protected. In order for that vision to be sustained, a community must steward it and pass it on.

For this reason, the biblical texts for a given Sunday reveal themselves to be the governing source for everything else in the worship. The images and themes of the word serve as the font for the events that occur even from the beginning of worship, so that greetings, invocations, calls to worship, opening psalms, hymns, and prayers all reflect the day's texts. The Bible is opened and out from its great wisdom pours the language of welcome and praise, lament and joy, prayer and even silence that all become the worship. Out from the words of Scripture comes the language of singing and preaching. The word of God is the bedrock of the worship.

Greeting and Singing in the Language of God's Word

To begin the assembly's worship with God's word sets the context and differentiates the Gathering from all other occasions of meeting. A sporting event begins with a national anthem; a concert, with the first violin tuning the orchestra. A trial in a courtroom begins with the words, "All rise." Church is not these. The Gathering words evoke that difference.

Assemblies that begin worship with the presider's Greeting, "The Lord be with you," followed by the people's response, "And also with you," echo the blessing between Boaz and his workers (Ruth 2:4). The mutual blessing between Boaz and the reapers in his fields is a model for us of the relationship of generosity Boaz shows in the story. By using the words of greeting from Ruth, the relationships among the people in the assembly are enlivened with the same generosity. It would be a good thing if the pastor made this clear from time to time so people could know the breadth and depth of the greeting.

In a similar way, the assembly hears the apostle Paul speaking through the ages where the words of greeting are "The grace of our Lord Jesus Christ, the love of God, and the communion of the Holy Spirit be with you all" (2 Cor. 13:13), with the people responding, "And also with you." Here, as well, language that evokes the triune God is set before the worshipers, announcing that whatever the season, whatever the day, the governing power is that of the Trinity.

Where the greeting or gathering is a Call to Worship, it may come in the form of a psalm or other language that echoes the Scripture readings for the day. The Presbyterian *Book of Common Worship*[2] offers, among others, these words for Gathering: "Our help is in the name of the LORD, / who made heaven and earth" (Ps. 124:8), or "This is the day that the LORD has made; / let us rejoice and be glad in it" (Ps. 118:24), or "O praise the LORD with me, / let us exalt God's name together" (Ps. 34:3). Using a psalm needs to be done with care. Psalm 103 ("Bless the LORD, O my soul, / and all that is within me, bless God's holy name") suits the Call to Worship while Psalm 22 ("My God, my God, why have you forsaken me? / Why so far from saving me, so far from the words of my groaning?") would not, unless the season is very penitent (as with our case study from Ash Wednesday). Other considerations in using a psalm for the Call include:

- The psalm is sung or spoken by the whole assembly and works best in the Gathering if it is in the plural voice: "God is our refuge and strength, / a very present help in trouble" (Psalm 46). If the psalm begins in the singular voice, does it move into a plural? "How dear to me is your dwelling, / O LORD of hosts! . . . Happy are they who dwell in your house! / They will always be praising you . . ." (Ps. 84:1, 4).

- The psalm should fit the tone of the day in keeping with the preaching texts and in that way serving the preaching. "You are to be praised, O God, in Zion; / to you shall vows be fulfilled. . . . Happy are they whom you choose and draw to your courts to dwell there! / They will be satisfied . . ." (Ps. 65:1, 4). This expounds the joy of the people coming into the presence of a powerful God and would be appropriate on almost any Sunday.

- If a psalm is to be used, the presider and musician (cantor) might work toward singing it, because the psalter is a song-book. For churches that have not become accustomed to singing the appointed lectionary psalm as a response to the first reading, use of the psalm as a Call can be a fine way for the assembly to learn to sing the language of these ancient prayers.

For the word to permeate the liturgy, the Scripture texts—whether they adhere to a lectionary or are chosen by the preacher each week—serve as the starting point for choosing hymns. Scripture readings are amplified for the congregation when the music echoes and extends the images and themes of God's word, but this is true primarily for the hymn following the sermon. As church musician Mark Mummert writes:

> Music invokes the power of God to create something out of nothing: water where there was no water, praise where there was only fear of Pharaoh; and a merciful escape, proclamation of God's grace and mercy after ancient promises were fulfilled, and a revelation of future restoration after destruction when all the earth sings "Holy, holy, holy." The biblical witness assumes musical power, a power flowing from the power of the triune God, a power to change, gather, praise, proclaim, and propel into action. Music is a sign of God at work in the world. The conviction that the triune God revealed in the scriptures is a God who creates, sustains, and enlivens by audible means is, indeed, a sound theology.[3]

The Opening Hymn (or Gathering Song) has the primary task of unifying the people's breath. Its intent is to help the assembly move in a visceral way from being a collection of individuals to being one body. Hymns sing of myriad subjects suitable to the beginning of worship: morning joy ("When Morning Gilds the Skies"), seeing sisters and brothers in faith ("Dearest Jesus, at Your Word"), Holy Spirit ("Come and Fill Our Hearts," a Taizé chant based on Psalm 136:1), God's presence ("God Is Here!"), and sheer praise ("Shout to the Lord").[4] These hymns and others do not need to echo exactly the texts for the day, but thematically they should lead the assembly toward hearing the word,

If the congregation subscribes to a lectionary that is available to the assembly on a regular basis, the musicians may choose to emphasize a certain aspect of the word, even in the gathering music. If the Scripture for the Sunday is chosen by the preacher and is not available to the musicians in time to choose related music, the musicians may only have two options: (1) to offer new songs that they have practiced but which the assembly cannot participate in singing, or (2) to repeat hymns and songs the assembly already knows but which have no necessary connection either to the sermon text for that particular Sunday or to the tenor of the day. Unless the musicians have time to consider well ahead what music would most help to underscore the Scripture's imagery and themes, the music will either undermine the assembly's ability to sing or remain disconnected from the word and proclamation.[5]

Of course, the hymn should be appropriate to the day, but this is not impossible to work out. Along with the musician (and the worship committee), the preacher may choose hymns well ahead of time, trusting that if the focus is on God's word, whatever turns the sermon takes, the underlying point will be attended. When the hymn text sings the great themes of the lections, the sermon and hymns will, necessarily, serve the word by supporting each other.

Language in a hymn might inform the sermon, but using a hymn text in the sermon can be dangerous because it can easily become an excuse for the preacher to end the sermon with someone else's pretty language instead of one's own. Furthermore, tying the hymn text and sermon together too tightly may rob the assembly of its role. The singing is the assembly's prayer rather than the preacher's text. Hopefully, the assembly hears a proclamation of the good news in the sermon that the people affirm in song.

It is not to be expected that every song be somehow reminiscent of actual language in the texts. If the Sunday commemorates the martyrdom of Stephen, for example, Stephen does not need to be the subject of every hymn. Rather, focus on faithfulness, witness, trials and oppression, and on God's deliverance would be the thematic echoes found in the hymns.

Praying in the Language of God's Word

Just as the scriptural word serves as the basis for greeting, call to worship, and hymn choices, the language of Scripture finds its way into the prayers that gather the people. In churches that bring the assembly together with an Opening Prayer or a Prayer of the Day (called a "Collect" in earlier times), the prayer may call up images and themes from the day's texts, especially encapsulating the great themes of the Gospel text. This prayer is spoken by the presider to pull the assembly in toward the gathering itself and the meaning of the day. This prayer is not intended to imitate a jovial crowd-warming introduction to the worship but instead signals at the outset the critical matters that will be the substance of the service, including the sermon. This is not to say that the Prayer of the Day is a time to introduce sermon themes, but that by laying out the character of the Gospel text—and in so doing, also reminding the assembly of the place of a given Sunday in the liturgical calendar—the prayer turns the people toward the word of God.

The Prayer of the Day is ecumenical in that it can be shared. It is common to—and open to—everyone. Use of ancient prayers carries familiar language offered to the ecumenical church from ancestors whose words spoke so deeply in their time that the church has handed them on. The Holy Spirit works to create all prayer whether written or extemporaneous. Many ancient prayers are reworked over generations, finding their way into new worship books, shared across denominations. On Pentecost, for example, when the whole church celebrates its birth through the work of the Holy Spirit in wind and fire, the prayer from the Anglican *Book of Common Prayer* (*BCP*) is:

> O God, who on this day taught the hearts of your faithful people by send-
> ing to them the light of your Holy Spirit: Grant us by the same Spirit to have
> a right judgment in all things, and evermore to rejoice in his holy comfort;
> through Jesus Christ your Son our Lord, who lives and reigns with you, in the
> unity of the Holy Spirit, one God, for ever and ever. Amen.[6]

Notice the image of the Holy Spirit coming into the people just as in the story of Pentecost the "tongues of fire" appeared on each of them. The

Holy Spirit is imaged as light—an ancient way of understanding baptism as a Pentecost event, an "enlightenment" that animates faith. The plea of the prayer is for the Spirit to direct people to judicious choices and joy.

The *BCP* form of this prayer served as the source for the version used in *Evangelical Lutheran Worship* (*ELW*). The language—revised, yet maintaining its basic shape and substance—reminds the assembly week after week that faith is a gift nurtured and expressed by our ancestors and then given to us as it was given to them. None of us invents our faith from whole cloth. We do not have to be "creative" in our way of speaking of God. We are continually called to pour new wine into new wineskins, but the old words are made new by the newness of our lives, and so the old words still speak to us and feed us.

For churches that embrace extemporaneous prayer, the same can be said of gifts having been handed down. Where prayers are prized as spontaneous outpourings of the Holy Spirit, we can hear a shape and pattern and rhythm to the praying that, in its very form, reminds us of a structure that is taught from generation to generation. Spontaneous prayer, by the very shape it takes, its steady informality and immediate expression from the heart, resonates with the assembly because the nouns and verbs in their very arrangement, stories, characters, and journeys—even certain phrases that reoccur in cultural and theological groups—conjure up the faith. As with written prayer, the spontaneous prayer will do well to draw on the language and imagery of the text(s) for the day in order to lay them into the assembly's hearing at the beginning of the service. The assembly is, in this way, oriented by the word toward the word.

Case Study

The Scripture readings for Ash Wednesday raise up the specter of death and the ways in which God calls us to live in its presence: "the day of the LORD is coming . . . a day of darkness and gloom . . ." (Joel 2:1-2). God, who abounds in steadfast love, calls us to gather together, fast, leave our occupations, come where the priests are weeping and begging God to spare us, for we are always in danger of losing our way, turning our backs on our real treasure. This wealth of images can direct the worshipers—overtly or more subtly—to the sermon's focus.

I chose to use Psalm 51 to open the liturgy (either Psalm 51 or another psalm, litany, or hymn are appointed) because it contains the penitential plea of one who trusts that God will forgive: "Have mercy on me, O God, according to your steadfast love. . . . Create in me a clean heart, O God, / and renew a right spirit within me." These words feed right into the problematic creaturely "dustiness" that is human being. This is the place from which to begin Lent.

I could have chosen a hymn for a Gathering song in place of Psalm 51, in which case Psalm 51 would be used elsewhere, sung as a response to the reading from Joel or during the Imposition of Ashes. Given that the season of Lent is beginning, with the sermon focus on "rend your hearts," I looked for a hymn that captures the journey of Lent, the movement of lives into and out of wildernesses, the sure promise of God's help. A mid-twentieth-century text with a nineteenth-century Welsh tune in a minor key, "Bless now, O God, the journey that all your people make," fills all these needs.[7] As I continue to think about music for this liturgy, working closely with the musician(s), I try to vary the centuries, the ethnicity, and the mood of the hymn choices so that what comes through is the relationship of the song to the general themes of the day.

The Prayer of the Day for Ash Wednesday lays out the main themes of the texts, alerting the assembly to what it will hear in the reading and preaching. Consider this from *ELW*:

> Gracious God, out of your love and mercy you breathed into dust the breath of life, creating us to serve you and our neighbors. Call forth our prayers and acts of kindness, and strengthen us to face our mortality with confidence in the mercy of your Son, Jesus Christ, our Savior and Lord, who lives and reigns with you and the Holy Spirit, one God, now and forever. Amen.[8]

Where the Prayer of the Day is spontaneous, it can serve in this same function, utilizing the imagery and main theme of the gospel for this day.

The Gathering is a crucial time in the liturgy in which the elements all seek to orient the assembly toward God's word through music, greeting, and prayer that sets out the images and themes for the day. The Gathering brings the individuals together around the centrality of God's word, preparing for the next part of the worship that is hearing the Scripture texts, the word preached, the response of the assembly in song, possibly Confession of Faith, and then prayer for all the world.

Chapter 5

Word

He explained the scriptures to them.

> Then [Jesus] said to them, "Oh, how foolish you are, and how slow of heart
> to believe all that the prophets have declared! Was it not necessary that
> the Messiah should suffer these things and then enter into his glory?" Then
> beginning with Moses and all the prophets, he interpreted to them the
> things about himself in all the scriptures. (Luke 24:25-27)

After the stranger joins the two disciples on their walk to Emmaus, the
scriptures are addressed. The stranger points immediately to the word of
God as the appropriate place to turn when confronted with an existential
crisis. In the word is written everything pertaining to what occurs in our
world. For the two on the road, the "scriptures beginning with Moses
and all the prophets" provide perspective on the events that have been
happening of late in Jerusalem—or, as we would say, the events everywhere at all times.

Before the stranger launches into an interpretation of "these things,"
he speaks in riddles, asking the disciples a rhetorical question—"Was it not
necessary . . . ?"—because of course, in their state of heart and mind, they
could not have that vision. They could not see "necessity" in what had
taken place. This inability is a common human limitation. The two disciples
on the road are suffering and fearful because they are, in effect, struggling
with the problem of theodicy. So it is with human life. Having easy access

to ready answers for the problem of the existence of evil and pain is that we are always wrong, no matter how we explain it.

The stranger on the road was uniquely qualified to use the language of necessity. Along with the disciples, today's preacher must listen to him with deep humility. This stranger is, in fact, the Word. Preaching serves to do today what he did for the disciples on their journey: open up the Scriptures so that God's desire for creation is made known.

Fundamental to that task is honesty. Before the stranger begins to address the problem the disciples have been talking about, he tells them a truth about themselves: "Oh, how foolish you are!" In these words is a harsh mirror that the stranger must articulate because by doing so, he establishes his larger and deeper insight. One cannot determine another person's level of inability without having a greater vista from which to observe.

Indeed, *we* know that the stranger is the one who makes hearts burn and opens the eyes of the blind, so when we hear these words assessing the foolishness of his companions on the road, we know the stranger is speaking also of *our* foolishness, of the blindness of human beings whose dexterity in wringing meaning out of disparate experiences lacks consistency and profundity. It is possible to listen to the stranger's next words and believe them because this small phrase is the truth: "How foolish you are and slow . . . !" In the same way, when worship begins with an honest word about the assembly's need for the truth about itself, a space opens up in the midst of the people—even within each individual—in which hope may be received into the often harsh reality of the truth. Once you have heard your truth spoken, your vulnerability allows otherwise impossible transformations to come into being. Think of the response to Jesus from the woman at the well. She ran to her neighbors to say, "He told me everything I have ever done!" She could experience respect for and even awe of him because he knew her in a thorough and important way.

So it is with worship that speaks the whole truth. Honesty creates context for the preaching to fall upon open, even broken, hearts. It is not enough to begin and end with joy. There is sorrow in our lives. Along with triumph and accomplishment, human beings know misery, failure, guilt, and shame. These truthful depictions of human life need to be articulated with God's word and our own words, and when they are, we are readied to receive the interpretation about the Risen One told "in all the scriptures." Without truth, healing comes haltingly or not at all. When, on the road, the stranger speaks the truth—that his companions cannot fathom how to respond to Jesus' death and his purported appearance to the women—he opens Cleopas and the other disciple to a new awakening. Such is the power of the truth, especially when it is hard to swallow.

The Sunday assembly needs honesty about humanity in order for the interpretation of God's word to find a home. What is at issue here is balance between critique of human living and celebration of it, between cries of pain and those of joy. One without the other is not the truth.

The Scriptures Are Read Aloud

Our earlier discussion of Nehemiah 8 asserted that the word of God read aloud in the presence of the people is an event of God speaking. As such, the Scriptures should be proclaimed in the liturgy. The Scriptures are not merely homiletical jumping-off points but are the holy Word made manifest among us when the book opens and the good news pours out. Because the lectionary readings appointed for any given Sunday—but especially in the festival time of the calendar—are chosen to resonate with one another, they should all be read.[1] The word of God is not primarily or only for personal study or private devotion. It is the voice of the Lord, first heard and beloved by people who, for the most part, could not read.

Some preachers today insist that the people "just cannot handle" too many stories or images, that only one of the texts or only a portion of a text should be read. This perspective, while condescending, is also theologically suspect because the Scriptures are meant to be set next to each other in all their fullness. The stranger on the road to Emmaus had to begin with Moses and then speak of all the prophets in order to "interpret himself." So must we, adding the writings of the New Testament, as well. No one passage is enough. No one scripture text says everything. It is in their opposition and difference that the way of faith is revealed. Even when the preacher has settled on just one text or one portion of a text for the substance of the sermon, the people are best served by hearing all the lections for the day. Faith comes from what is heard.

It is always important to help the lectors (readers) do a superb job of proclaiming the word of God in the reading. They need to have the texts in hand well ahead of the worship service and be coached for pronunciation and emphasis. A good reading preaches the gospel with as much conviction as a sermon, while an inept reading can obscure the import. Some churches ask laypeople to read the first two lections with the preacher reading the Gospel in preparation for preaching. If the preacher reads the main preaching text, he or she is able to give appropriate emphases to important themes and words that have shaped the sermon. It has been assumed in many churches that the preaching text *is* the Gospel reading, but that is neither required nor even desirable. The good news may be just as evident in the Old Testament as in the New.

It has also come to be commonplace that the order in which texts should be read begins with the Old Testament,[2] then the epistle (or other second reading from Acts or Revelation), and finally the Gospel. If the preacher wants appropriate emphasis on certain words, she or he may read the text at issue and ask laity to read the other two. Another option—long the practice in Anglican churches—has laity read all three texts. The primary concern is that Scripture be read aloud and well.

Preaching Interprets the Word

When the companions turn to the stranger with intrigue over his knowledge of them and face the truth of their situation (their misunderstanding and foolishness), the stranger *then* can interpret "to them the things about himself in all the scriptures," for this is what they need in order to continue on their journey. By telling us the stranger interpreted the scriptures as referring to himself, the writer of Luke signals that it is Jesus who has appeared on the road. He opens up the scriptures so that their interpretation brings light into darkness, hope into despair. This is preaching.

Just as on the road to Emmaus, preaching in worship today interprets the Scriptures so that what was written long ago is revealed as the very crux of present-day life. Past and present time are linked *through* the remembrance, the *anamnesis*, that comes when two or three gather in the presence of the Word. In our time, we look both backwards to Christ's life with us in order to set the present in the context of the promised future. We *remember* in order to know God's steadfastness today and in the coming time.

When we interpret the Scriptures in order to understand our lives in the light of the Risen One, we engage with "all the scriptures" as did the stranger on the road. This does not mean that the sermon will unpack each of the readings, but, rather, that whatever the sermon chooses as the heart of its concern (the *hertzpunkt*) that heart will express the core of the good news. It is not enough that we focus on one phrase or even one text, unless we have taken into account—so as to see it in the context of—all the rest of the Scriptures. Once the contradictions have been broached (such as life arisen from death!), a way can be seen that embraces necessary paradox.

Responding to the Sermon

Proclamation of God's word in preaching necessarily calls for the assembly's response. In churches that do not hold weekly communion (for whom the worship pattern is either a Service of the Word or Frontier Revival), the assembly's response to the preached word is to express faith through offering gifts, singing, praying, and perhaps affirming faith. This might be called the third section of the Service of the Word, for this pattern is Gathering, Word, Response, Sending.

For assemblies that include the meal (Gathering, Word, Meal, Sending), the response to the sermon is also expression of the faith engendered by the preaching: singing a hymn, offering prayer, confessing faith, and sharing the peace of Christ. These actions are directly tied to the preached word as we shall see in this section.

A hymn sung after the sermon serves as a prayer through which the congregation finds unity as a body through rhythmic breathing and words sung in unison. Wherever hymns are placed in the service, they should either echo language and themes found in the Scripture texts or in the primary text on which the preacher will focus the sermon or serve a function such as gathering the people, allowing contemplative time, sending, or perhaps celebrating a particular time of day. In this way, the assembly is offered yet another venue for hearing and expressing—and being gathered into—the word of God.

The logic of the location of the prayers at this point has to do with the fact that after Gathering, the assembly hears God's Word read and preached and then, bolstered by the revelation of Christ's presence through the word, the people respond with a proclamation of faith and prayers for the whole world. Referring to this as a "logic" or a reasoned progression of events means to focus on the unfolding of faith through word: after the word is opened, the assembly has the capacity to respond with concern for others. God's powerful presence, the indwelling Holy Spirit resident as Word, visits the people with the necessary compassion to respond in petitions of thanks and pleading.

If a confession of faith follows the sermon, its placement reinforces the assertion that "faith comes from what is heard, and what is heard comes through the word of Christ" (Rom. 10:17). We do not necessarily arrive at church on Sunday morning full of faith, but we are eager for the word that will renew us. It is the preaching that makes possible the confession of faith, because the confession is a summary of all that is written in the Holy Scriptures. Whether the language of the confession is the ancient Apostles' or Nicene Creeds or, as in some denominations, written anew periodically to refresh the hearing of the believers, it means to unite the body in language that encapsulates the entire story. Churches that omit the creed (some historically have done so; others more recently) cite its divisive character, formed at the Council of Nicea in 325 c.e. to clarify the trinitarian relationship and to distinguish orthodox believers from the heretics. But speaking a confession is, for many, a unifying action because, through the complexity of the assertions ("I believe in the resurrection of the body and life everlasting . . ."), the body of Christ claims the mystery together. When a confession of faith is used, it can serve the preaching by giving the preacher a body of language that comes to be familiar and symbolically rich to the assembly. It can also, as a response to the preaching, reintroduce large, even mythic images following words in the sermon that may have brought the focus closer to home. The creed, then, brings the convictions of the whole catholic church into the hearing of the assembly.

In churches where Intercessory Prayers (also called Intercessions or the Prayers of the People, among others) follow the creed, the assembly offers up its concern for the needs of the world. These prayer petitions—sometimes spoken as one long prayer of thanks and beseeching, sometimes broken into petitions of thanks or pleading with assembly responses—mean to name the breadth and depth of the Christian witness. If the preaching has stirred the compassion of the congregation to deepened gratitude for God's actions of redemption and new life, the assembly will be drawn to prayer for the church in all the world, for believers of all faiths, for the needs of the nations and world leaders, for refugees from war, for people who are hungry, for those who have no homes, for the sick, the dying, the lonely—all because the word of God has so filled them with conviction about God's goodness that all joys and sorrows will be lifted up in certainty that God listens and will act.

Intercessions that focus solely on the congregation's own problems or local members' needs fail to offer the bigger heart that the preaching means to foster. Leaving time in the Prayers of the People for the assembly to voice particular concerns can be a remarkable time of cohesion, giving everyone the opportunity to pray *with* each other. It is not a good time to announce a death or a piece of gossip that will leave people reeling. But this can be avoided by announcing at the beginning of the worship the people for whom prayer will be made or by encouraging a prayer form with a simple structure: "We pray for Charles . . . for all churches in China . . . for Jean as she awaits surgery . . . for students as they return to school . . ."

The prayers may be offered by a different layperson each Sunday or by persons who have been called out for their prayer leadership. When the preacher gives the prayers, it is a great temptation to turn them into a footnote to the sermon. Hearing the Intercessions in the different voices of the congregation gives the assembly a little glimpse of what prayer and being church means to that person. It is a way for the preacher to hear the real concerns of the assembly. These prayers both serve and are served by the preaching in the way through which they open up the members of the church to each other. We learn what is on other's hearts.

It may require regular coaxing and teaching about prayer to help members of the congregation take responsibility for the Intercessions.[3] At the least, begin by gathering a group together to look at the purpose of intercessory prayer. Remind them that the pray-er speaks for the whole assembly with the plural pronoun *we*. The prayers most successfully will name everyone who stands in need of prayer that day. Give each prayer leader an outline for the prayers, including the categories of prayer concerns that call up the breadth of God's mercy for the entire world:

- for the whole church

- for all people of faith (including non-Christian faiths)

- for creation, creatures, plants, and animals

- for justice and peace in all nations, for leaders and communities

- for the poor, ill, dying, frightened, lonely

- for all who suffer in any way from physical, mental, and spiritual troubles

- for the local congregation and special concerns

Naturally, these are categories. When all these concerns have been named—being as specific as possible, for example, by naming nations, naming specific environmental worries in particular places, naming the hope for a good and safe journey for the youth group—the next petition may be an invitation for the assembly to voice petitions. This can be done by saying simply, "for all the concerns of this assembly named aloud or silently at this time." By then keeping silence, those who wish to name additional individuals and conditions about which they have been in prayer will do so.

After this open prayer, the final petition may be thanksgiving for all the saints who have gone before us. Here can be named those who have just died in the congregation or community and whose commemoration days in the larger church are approaching in the coming week. Nothing didactic should be said about the ancestors named, such as a plea that God make us to be like them. The prayers conclude with reference to trust in God's mercy toward all for whom the prayer has been made.

Where assemblies have begun to "pass the peace," as it is called, it follows right after the prayers and can be seen as a direct response to the preached word. Because of the good news of the Risen Christ, we pray for all the world and then enact that expression of solidarity with others far away from us by turning to the ones close at hand with a blessing: "The peace of Christ be with you," or similar words. It can be a time of profound healing for some in the assembly, a formal and bounded way to begin to break through a disagreement. Shy people can be comforted to know there is no need for extended conversation during the peace; only to extend peace. The response to the preached word, then, ends in peace. This is the appropriate goal of God's word: to move us toward peace with others.

Case Study

The liturgy on Ash Wednesday is classically the structure of Gathering, Word, Ashes, Meal, and Sending. The disciplines of Lent themselves are a focus for worship on Ash Wednesday. Following the sermon and the responsive hymn, the presider invites the assembly into Lenten observance, leads them in a Confession of Sin, and then offers the Imposition of Ashes on each person's forehead. It is a very sober time, and in keeping with that solemnity, the sermon will gauge its tone toward the serious nature of the day's reminder that we are made of dust and return to dust.

The intercessions, hymns, and the particular ritual action of receiving ashes all contributed to driving home the fact that on this day, the church openly faces death. As mentioned in the previous chapter, Psalm 51 might be sung between the reading of Joel and the epistle. If the service begins with singing Psalm 51, then Psalm 103:8-14 would be used after the Joel reading ("Bless the LORD, O my soul, / and all that is within me, bless God's holy name").

To announce the Gospel reading, the congregation sang its greeting to the Word. Because this beginning of Lent is a subdued occasion, as in many churches, the assembly does not sing "Alleluia." In fact, on the prior Sunday, Transfiguration Sunday, the ritual action of "burying" the Alleluia is enacted in many churches. For the time of Lent, the liturgical responses and hymns will not contain that word. Instead, on Ash Wednesday, the assembly greets the word of God with these words from the Joel reading: "Return to the LORD, your God, / who is gracious and merciful, slow to anger, and abounding in steadfast love."

On Ash Wednesday, the sermon most fruitfully revolves around the purpose of Lent, since this day begins the season. The preacher might spend a little time helping the assembly understand Lent, especially to say that it is not merely for giving up something dear but for finding a discipline that can strengthen desire for the things that are truly enriching. The sermon may invite the assembly members to wear the ashes for the rest of the day as a sign of their faith or to wash them off on the way out in order not to be displaying their piety (in the spirit of the Gospel reading's admonitions against hypocrisy).

Foremost in my mind on such a ponderous day was the possibility of the sermon being an anchor for the meaning of the ashes: preparing the assembly to receive them as a sign of the incarnation as well as decay, a sign of our equality before God, a sign of our acknowledgment that life is fleeting and hard but that God's power overcomes all ultimate pointlessness. Everything rests on the dust and ashes on this day.

Preparation for the sermon also involved revisiting the actual preparation for imposition of ashes. Traditionally, the palms from the previous years' Palm Sunday liturgy are burned the night before Ash Wednesday, called Shrove Tuesday, Fat Tuesday, *Fastnacht*, and other ethnic and cultural names since it is the time of celebration (think Mardi Gras) when Christian households clean out the flour, eggs, fats, and sweets from the kitchen and turn to fasting for Lent.[4] Tuesday night is for eating doughnuts or pancakes.

But it is also, then, for burning the palms and sifting them for use the next day. Congregation members may be invited to bring the palms they have saved from the previous year. And it is always a good idea for the pastor to set aside leftover palms on Palm Sunday to be burned the next year.

Hymns appropriate to the word that calls us to "rend our hearts" and "return to the LORD" invite hymn texts that speak in the first-person singular: "Be thou my vision" or "Change my heart, O God."[5] Lent is traditionally the time of preparation for baptism, so the focus is on the individual learning the faith, taking the Apostle's Creed to heart since it was and remains the substance of the renunciation and confession prior to the washing in churches that adhere to word-and-sacrament liturgical shape. Hymns that speak in first-person plural contain larger themes, more focused on God's work on and in us than on our experience of God's place in our individual lives: "By gracious powers" or "Great God, your love has called us here."[6] We chose "Out of the depths I cry to you, O Lord" for this hymn responds to the sermon by confessing great poverty of soul: "Do not regard my sinful deeds. / Send me the grace my spirit needs; / without it I am nothing."[7] The first and fourth stanzas speak in first-person singular; the second and third, in plural voice.

Special to this liturgy is its stunning call to the assembly to take on the disciplines described in the readings, especially in Joel and Matthew. In order for the people to embrace the call, we must begin by confessing our inabilities. Directly from that confession, we receive ashes of our mortality. The meaning of the sermon's focus on rending the heart is here represented in a visual, tactile manner. The liturgical action inscribes on the body the very substance of life and death.

During the imposition of ashes, while individuals are coming forward to receive them, we considered using the Latvian folk tune based on Psalm 137 that begins: "Once we sang and danced with gladness, once delight filled every breath; / now we sit among the ashes, all our dreams destroyed by death" and ends "Come, O Christ, among the ashes, come to wipe our tears away . . ."[8] Instead, we used the rich Taizé chant "Bless the Lord, My Soul . . ." until everyone had returned to a seat. "Once we sang and danced . . ." was used during the distribution because its minor key set together with words of joy (danced, sang) embodies the meal of the broken Lord giving joy.

The prayers of the people (primarily intercessions) do not simply echo the themes from the sermon, but they do consider the substance of the liturgical day (especially at such an important time as the beginning of Lent). The prayers are most appropriate when they cast a wide net over the needs of the world and then in some petitions name a specific place, concern, or person.[9]

The final movement of the Word portion of the liturgy is the passing of the peace. The peace is, in some ways, a culmination of the sermon, for even Augustine taught that the end of preaching is to increase love for God and love for neighbor. The prayers and the peace serve as a pivot between Word and Meal, enacting a response to the word read and preached. In that way the prayers and peace serve the word, and on Ash Wednesday in particular, they express what the ashes have caused the assembly to see: the great debt we owe, the huge love Christ has made possible, and the task of peace-making in our midst. The prayers and peace, having been engendered by the word, are served by the preaching. The next chapter will focus on the Meal as the visible word.

Chapter 6

Meal

Their eyes were opened in the breaking of the bread.

> As they came near the village to which they were going, he walked ahead
> as if he were going on. But they urged him strongly, saying, "Stay with us,
> because it is almost evening and the day is now nearly over." So he went
> in to stay with them. When he was at the table with them, he took bread,
> blessed and broke it, and gave it to them. Then their eyes were opened, and
> they recognized him; and he vanished from their sight. They said to each
> other, "Were not our hearts burning within us while he was talking to us on
> the road, while he was opening the scriptures to us?" (Luke 24:28-32)

As we have seen, a quintessential image of the place of God's word in the
worship life of the church comes from the Emmaus story. As they reach
the village, the stranger moves to leave the disciples. Their desire to spend
more time with him calls him to remain with them. Notice that *they* urge
him to stay. We do not know their motivation. We only know that this
story shows us disciples who, after hearing the scriptures opened to them,
find themselves inviting the stranger to come in.

Remarkably, then, this stranger becomes the host. Without an expla-
nation in the story for why this should happen, we are told that he takes
the bread and speaks a blessing over it. As he breaks and distributes it,
those at the table receive insight into his identity, and then he suddenly
vanishes. The word for "their eyes *were opened*" is *diēnoichthēsan*, which

includes the sense of a complete and thorough change in their vision that happened *to* them (passive verb) in a one-time event (aorist verb tense). Their eyes—their ability to comprehend—suddenly acquire a new vision. They see who the stranger is. They understand that what the women have learned is somehow true. Because he vanishes, they have no means for grilling him further on this mystery, but they are left with perceptible burning hearts.

New Vision Is God's Doing

The birth of the church in this story begins with a reasoned examination of the scriptures so that God's word can illuminate the present times. Then that realization is made physically palpable by a gathering at table, breaking bread, being warmed—burning!—with a realization that is beyond words. This is a picture of worship that is grounded in the centrality of God's word because no part of the action is complete without the others. Most of all, none of this would happen were it not for the creating, redeeming, and sustaining Word of God present in the people—the body of Christ—and in the holy book, the baptismal waters, and at the table.

If the Emmaus story is indicative of the relationship between the stranger and the disciples, we are assured in the disciples' remarks to each other that it is Jesus who comes to us, makes our hearts burn as he interprets the Scriptures, and opens our eyes as he breaks the bread at table. It is not we who muster up our resources and, without any assistance from the Risen One, ask him to "stay with us." Rather, before we even know what we are feeling or seeing, something within us is fired with desire just as the disciples' hearts burned on the road through Jesus' opening of the scriptures. And then, it is Jesus' own offering of himself—the breaking of bread, the giving of his body—that gives us vision.

We do not acquire the vision of Jesus' identity on our own. We do not have the wherewithal to accomplish that work, whether as individuals, congregations, denominations, or the universal church. Instead, we are acted upon by the one who interprets the things about himself in all the Scriptures and then takes, blesses, breaks, and gives to us his own body.

The church in a majority of its denominations has maintained the practice of the weekly meal—the Lord's Supper, Holy Communion, Eucharist, are only some of its many names—all of which involve bread and wine (or the juice of grapes) over which the church gives thanks and eats. More and more, communions that have taken to heart the insights of recent liturgical renewal are urging congregations to return to the meal practice. It is an embrace of the eye-opening pattern we have been looking at in this Emmaus story: God's word, opened, pulls the people toward God's meal shared.

Offering

In preparation for the meal, the people whose ears have been opened by the word and whose hearts have responded with prayer for the world are now given an opportunity for offering of self, time, and possessions, making the people themselves—the body of Christ—another visible sign of God's word. When the gifts are assembled and brought forward, a prayer is said giving thanks for the bounty. Where the meal itself is not included in the worship, this offering time may be understood more explicitly as an expanded response to the hearing of the word. In some congregations it may be an invitation for individuals to rededicate themselves to a changed life. It may be a time for individual prayer and healing. It may have been deepened by the sermon.

All in all, the time of offering is a delicate and dangerous moment because it is fraught with the possibility that we misunderstand our response to God's bounty. Did the sermon set us on edge so that guilt compels us? Did the sermon thrill us with thanks and make us eager to share? Are we giving something to God? Are we pledging our possessions to the welfare of others? Are we paying dues? Do we know and understand that bringing forward the financial gifts is an act that binds us to our sisters and brothers? If the bread and wine is carried to the table along with the money, do we know that it is not *we* who bring the bread and wine, the body and blood, but Jesus' own self incarnate in the elements bound to our place on earth, identified with the bread of our locality and the wine of the nearby vineyards? The Offering in its best form may be a dedication or rededication of ourselves. It may afford us the concrete steps we need in order to understand the import of our lives lived fully dependent on God. Ritually, it reinforces week after week that we do not need to hoard and that our lives are, like that of the broken bread, best lived in giving away. If the sermon has said this, the Offering makes it visible and personal.

Setting the Table

When the holy meal is part of the liturgy, the money offerings may be brought forward while the table is set for the meal. The chalice or cups are brought out in the same manner as one sets a dining table at home, expecting the guests to arrive soon. Setting the table may be understood as somewhat analogous to the Prayer of the Day that "collects" the assembly in preparation for hearing the audible word. The table setting prepares the assembly to see and receive the visible word. During this time, a hymn might be sung to joyfully welcome the meal, using the imagery of the meal, of the community itself, and of gratitude for the gifts of bread and wine. While the hymn might contain reference to larger themes from the word read and preached, the meal needs more prominently to speak of the gifts of God, and it is that which the table-setting hymn will celebrate.

Praying at the Table

Where the meal is offered, a prayer is said over the food, echoing the stranger's blessing over the bread in the house at Emmaus: ". . . he took bread, blessed and broke it, and gave it to them . . ." The roots of this blessing lie in Jewish *berakah*—the blessing over cup and then bread—with a closing doxology, given in gratitude for what is at hand. This prayer recalls the blessing of God at every meal and for whatever else one encounters that is worthy of thanks: "Bless you, O God, Creator of the universe, who gives us bread [beauty, song, air, water, friends, a daughter, a son, a family, this crop, this good outcome of a problem . . .]." The bread and wine of the meal is blessed by the one who presides at worship in words that give thanks for all God has done.

The earliest of documents describing what that blessing may have been in the early church is in the *Didache*.[1] It is a prayer of thanksgiving and pleading. It blesses God for the food that is given. The pattern of thanksgiving names the gifts through which God's glory is revealed. By way of giving thanks, then, the steadfastness of God's attention to the people's needs is praised through the "holy vine" of King David and the servant Jesus, and through the gifts of food and drink. The prayer has three sections: the first and second give thanks for the cup and the bread; the third blesses the holy name that has come to tabernacle (reside) in the assembly itself. Other traditions may alter the order of these thanksgivings or offer a trinitarian pattern giving thanks for the Creator and creation, for the Son who redeems, and for the Holy Spirit who abides in God's people and in God's gifts.

Some churches craft a new prayer of thanksgiving periodically, seasonally, or every Sunday, bringing into the prayer the concerns of the day and the themes and language of the lections. Those who adhere to the ancient prayer forms that focus on thanksgiving for the Trinity see this structure as upholding the substance of the meaning of the Word itself. In either pattern, through the one who presides over the meal, the gathered people pray gratitude in the way of family "grace" said at home.

Where Meal follows Word, the bread and wine make visible the otherwise invisible, audible word of God. Where there is thanksgiving, especially using the word of God, remembering the deeds of God's gracious and merciful presence through the ages and in the persons of Father, Son, and Holy Spirit, the recitation of salvation history in biblical images reminds the assembly not only of past events but of the ongoing work that God is effecting in the world.

Feeding the Body

The marvel of this meal lies in large measure as a sign of the absolute equality of all people in God's eyes. Each of us approaches the table with outstretched hands, empty hands, equally in need of sustenance. Each of us receives the same food, a piece of bread, a sip of wine. This little meal lifts up the lowly and pulls down the mighty so that we are ritually and tangibly shown to ourselves as equally needy before God.

The meal is a visible sign of the Word, giving abundantly to each person without prejudice, without judgment, without discrimination. The meal is a sign of the feast to come when God's reign tears down walls and allows us to kneel or stand together before the throne. But even more, it is an image of the justice God wills for us in our own world at the present time, proclaimed in the preaching and available at the table.

In its most elemental way, the meal serves the preaching by visually representing a vision of the kingdom or realm of God. The preaching ought to have named that realm as one in which all people are created in the image of God, all people are called to God's mercy and grace, and all people stand equally under God's judgment.

Case Study

The Ash Wednesday sermon, by building up an image of ashes and the green life thrusting through layers of deadness, means to level the pride of all who cling to inequalities among people. We live daily with the awful truth of death and disappointments, and we all are promised equally, in the body of Christ, the strength to push through the coarse blackness.

Coming to the table as individuals who are equal and yet each uniquely vital to the one body makes us whole.

During the setting of the table, the congregation sang the old nineteenth-century hymn by Will L. Thompson, "Softly and Tenderly Jesus Is Calling": "Come home, come home! You who are weary, come home."[2] Having been reminded by the sermon's images of thick dust and ashes on this liturgical day, it seemed fitting to let the assembly sink into the softness of a tender Jesus who acknowledges weariness and offers home. The table is home. The meal is home where the brothers and sisters gather.

The Prayer of Thanksgiving over the meal for Ash Wednesday[3] in many of our churches gives praise and thanks to the God for creating heaven and earth, saving earth from floods, bringing the Israelites to safety . . . for the words and deeds of Jesus, for his death and resurrection, for the Spirit "poured out on all nations." It includes the Words of Institution and then, remembering Jesus' Passover, asks for the Spirit's revelation in the breaking of the bread, for new life, for a burning sense of justice . . . ending with praise for God, the Holy Trinity. During the distribution of the bread and wine, the assembly sang "Come down, O Love divine; seek thou this soul of mine and visit it with thine own ardor glowing."[4] These are words from a fifteenth-century poet. When an assembly is normally given to singing more contemporary, less arcane language, with modern or "global" rhythms, it can be a very pleasing way to enter solemnity by engaging with terms like "thine own ardor" that suggest an era other than our own. The ashes are for all time, all people. This hymn says that in another form, just as the sermon meant to speak of the eternal, ultimate power of God's creative force.

The meal ends simply: the food is put away, the table cleared just as we would do in our dining rooms and kitchens. All that is left is for the assembly to be sent on its way. That is the subject of the next chapter.

Chapter 7

Sending

They told how he had been made known to them.

> That same hour they got up and returned to Jerusalem; and they found the
> eleven and their companions gathered together. They were saying, "The
> Lord has risen indeed, and he has appeared to Simon!" Then they told what
> had happened on the road, and how he had been made known to them in
> the breaking of the bread. (Luke 24:33-35)

The day was dark, nearly over. By the time they had gathered at table
and the stranger had taken the bread, blessed, broken it, and given it to
them, it was even later. But they were caught up in the realization that
their hearts burned on the road when he spoke about the scriptures. Now,
with their eyes "opened," they return at once to Jerusalem to seek out the
other disciples and report amazing experiences. Simon, too, has seen the
Lord, and those who came from Emmaus recognized this same Lord "in
the breaking of the bread." The disciples are "broken open." Their eyes
are unsealed. They hurry to share the news.

And the news is that in broken bread they have seen the Lord. Sometimes
it is worthwhile to notice what Scripture says in plain, even literal, terms
in order to see the value in it. To see Christ *in* broken bread is also to see
Christ *as* broken bread. The focus here is *broken*. The Risen One is known
by the disciples of Jesus' time and the disciples of our own time as one who
is broken apart in order to be given away. While other appearances of the

Risen Lord—to Mary in the garden, to the Twelve hiding in a closed room, to Simon—yielded other identities for the Risen One, at the table in Emmaus, the stranger who accompanied the disciples on the road becomes the Christ in broken bread.

Bread is a wondrously apt metaphor for the Risen Christ. It is elemental in many cultures as a staple of the diet, based in grain (or rice), mixed with water, baked, broken, and shared. It can be many shapes and densities. It sustains life. When we hear that Jesus identified himself with bread in the profound and mysterious words, "This is my body . . ." we are brought into the presence of a fundamental paradox. Bread, which is a product of human technology, is also named as the Lord's own self. To behold bread, in the context of the body of Christ gathered for the meal, is to stand in the place of ultimate contradiction. The body of Christ is shared with the body of Christ. Each has its own contour and texture, but the manner of eating—breaking and distributing—is the image of the assembly's own self-giving.

Again, we see that the Word of God is even at the heart of this central gift. We would not see the bread that is broken at the meal *as* the Risen Christ in our midst were it not for the command of Jesus to eat this bread because it *is* his body. It is crucial that the disciples report this phenomenal realization to their friends. Then, as we know, the meal continued to be enacted—the people gathered, the bread broken and distributed. It is one of the fundamental ways we know who we are as Christ's followers. But we only know the bread by the word of God.

The last action of worship is yet another way of enacting the meal. The church is broken and given away in the Sending: the distribution of the body of Christ out into the world. The body of Christ is, again, broken apart to be food for the life of the world. The primary breaking happens at the table as a sign of the continued breaking throughout the week until the scattered grains are gathered once again around the word and the table. At the end of worship, the people are sent out with a blessing.

Participants in the worship are sent to their homes and work and study, to the pursuits of childhood and of old age alike. Whatever one's vocation, the church proclaims God's presence in the world through that work and that child of God. The announcement of God's presence is made by the very fact of liturgical gathering and being sent. This is important to consider so that the worship is allowed to be its own virtue rather than merely an energizer for the "real" mission that lies outside the liturgical space.[1]

In *Sent and Gathered: A Worship Manual for a Church in Mission*, Clayton Schmit writes of the Sending as "the pivotal moment when worship turns from adoration to action."[2] Although it is a small portion of the worship, it is rightly named as pivotal. The moment of Sending is also delicate for this reason: If the mission of the church—to live as God's people in service—is ignored, the church becomes too insular. If the mission *as service* is regarded as primary, the presence of God in word and sacraments is relegated to a secondary role.

It may be best to think of the Sending as the movement from one of God's missions to another, from being gathered as the body of Christ to being dispersed as the body of Christ. Both are actions and both are adoration. We do not want to regard the worship itself as inaction, as an inert means by which the participant finds his or her "battery charged" in order to then go out and do the things that really matter. In the Sending, the several parts each contribute to bringing the Word into the moment of dispersal.

Commissioning

Some members of the assembly may take the leftover bread and wine to those who are sick or for other reasons were unable to join in worship. The shut-ins will hear one or more of the Scripture readings and a summary of the sermon. They will be told that in the thanksgiving over the bread and wine, the assembly remembered God's gifts of creation and Jesus who came for our liberation from sin and sorrow and the Holy Spirit who resides with us. In this way, their unity with the body of Christ will be brought tangibly to them through their sisters and brothers who bear the Word of God, bread of life, and cup of salvation. These lay ministers are trained so that they see themselves in the long lineage of deacons whose very task of mercy this has been through centuries. In the commissioning, these ministers are handed the bread and wine and a prayer may be said for their mission. In a similar way others who will leave for particular work on behalf of the church (such as missionaries, youth workers, chaplains) may also be singled out at this point for a special charge and prayer.

Announcements

The sending of persons for particular missions is an appropriate time to remind the entire assembly of actions in the coming week in which they may wish to participate. The announcements should be kept pointed, interesting, important, and short. While every congregation will grow accustomed to hearing the announcements at a certain time in the service, it may be helpful to think about the substance of the announcements as invitations to service in the church or on behalf of others. As an intentional part of the Sending, the announcements can fill the assembly with concrete ideas about what a life of dedicated faith, hope, and love might look like, what a life formed by the Word of God and articulated by the preaching might entail. The worship committee might consider bringing to the congregation's attention a need in the community that could prompt a response of the whole congregation working together using the Lenten disciplines of prayer, fasting, and almsgiving.

Concluding Prayer

A brief final prayer may conclude the commissioning and announcements, giving thanks for the opportunities to serve, reiterating the themes for the day from the liturgical season, the focus of the sermon as it relates to the work ahead of the assembly, or the hope that is given in Christ Jesus. This prayer should be clearly distinguished from the benediction or blessing and the dismissal, and it may be most helpful to think about it in the form of a classic collect: address to God, thanksgiving (for those who serve, for the work we have been given), petition (for those who are commissioned, for the congregation in its gathering and its daily life), and conclusion.

Benediction or Blessing

Immediately following the prayer, the presider gives the blessing or benediction to reaffirm the sure and certain presence of the life-giving God for the assembly as it leaves for the week. The presider blesses the assembly to let the last words of the gathering be words that speak of God's presence. It may be Aaron's blessing from Numbers 6:24-26: "The LORD bless you and keep you. The LORD's face shine on you with grace and mercy. The LORD look upon you with favor and give you peace. Amen." Other blessings echo trinitarian metaphors: "The God of steadfastness and encouragement grant you to live in harmony with one another, in accordance with Christ Jesus. Amen. / The God of hope fill you with all joy and peace in believing, so that you may abound in hope by the power of the Holy Spirit. Amen. / The God of all grace bless you now and forever. Amen."[3] Or more simply: "May the God of hope fill you with all joy and peace in believing, so that you may abound in hope by the power of the

Holy Spirit. Alleluia! Amen."[4] The benediction or blessing is not about what the people have to do once they have left the worship but about what God is going to continue doing in each person's life every day. This is a vital distinction because the blessing is not the same as a charge.

To give a blessing is to enact performative utterance, so to say the words, "The LORD bless . . ." is to make blessing happen. This is the appropriate role of the presider who has opened the liturgy with a greeting, offered prayer, made the Scriptures to be read, preached, prayed over the bread and wine, given the meal away to all the needy, and now blesses. This is the calling of someone who is ordained, set apart to oversee the gathering of the people. It is entirely appropriate that the one who has presided over the beginning of the worship—the one who preached, as well—is the one who gives the final blessing and concludes the time.

Charge

In place of a blessing or in addition to it, the assembly may hear a "charge" based in Scripture that reminds them of their individual responsibilities through the coming days, particularly as the lections for the day or the sermon have emphasized certain concerns. A presider using the *Book of Common Worship* of the Presbyterian Church (U.S.A.) might charge the assembly: "Go out into the world in peace. Love the Lord your God with all your heart, with all your soul, with all your mind; and love your neighbor as yourself."[5] Other words might be these: "As God's own, clothe yourselves with compassion, kindness, and patience, forgiving each other as the Lord has forgiven you, and crown all these things with love, which binds everything together in perfect harmony."[6]

Sending Song and Dismissal

The Sending song, as with earlier hymns, may suggest the language of the word read and preached, but its primary task is to bring the assembly's voice to a final thanksgiving for the feast of God's word and sacramental presence, praise for God's gifts and for the ways in which varied vocations express our faith. The song here is lively, joyous, and rich with the full expression of the day's celebration.

When the presider dismisses us, we are "sent" rather than simply scattering. We leave with purpose. For many congregations, a final dismissal may be: "Go in peace; remember the poor" (or "Go in peace; Christ is with you") to which the assembly replies, "Thanks be to God." The formality of such an ending makes a clear boundary for the liturgy. Now it is over. Now it is time to depart.

Sometimes it may seem that the Sending portion of the liturgy is so small it is barely noticeable. But there is another way to think of the shortness of the Sending. Considering all that has been said—in the word of God read and preached, the Response of the assembly, the prayers, the bread blessed and broken, the image of the body of Christ receiving the body of Christ—it might be more appropriate to see the Sending as too long, no matter what it contains.

The people are sent to live *in* God's word as it has been expressed in the whole worship event: Scripture reading, preaching, responses, prayer, and song. In being sent, the assembly enacts the paradox of the gathering itself, for the Word that gathers also inevitably and necessarily disperses. The members of the assembly belong to each other and to God in order to be given away for the sake of the world. The Sending begets more preaching through the witness of those who know the mercy and promises of God. This is especially apparent in that the "preaching" is not words alone but daily living in response to the needs of others.

Case Study

In keeping with the theological sensibility of a short Sending rite, I chose to end the liturgy simply with the Aaronic blessing—"The Lord bless you and keep you . . ."—which is an entirely fitting reminder that even during the season of Lent the primary identity of God is the One Who Watches Over You. Appropriate to Ash Wednesday is the sending hymn "Eternal Lord of love, behold your church / walking once more the pilgrim way of Lent, / led by your cloud by day, by night your fire, / moved by your love and toward your presence bent . . ."[7] It conjures the image of the Lenten journey—the pathway through the ashes—that Ash Wednesday ushers in.

Finally, the brief words of Dismissal are, "Go in peace; Christ is with you" to which the assembly responds: "Thanks be to God." For a day on which so much has been heard and experienced, with the church coming forward both for ashes and for bread and wine, the less said at the end, the better. The primary task of the Sending in this service was to give the blessing, sing a reminder of the great images of God's pilgrim journey with the people all through the ages, and make a final promise of communion in Christ. Whatever the assembly members take with them from the worship service on Ash Wednesday, it must be both ashes and mercy.

Serving the Word

The story of Emmaus is not a description of an event that has been gener-ated, created, or manipulated by the disciples on the road or by those who have gathered around the table. They did not say to themselves, "Let us find a way to manufacture a relationship with this Jesus whom we have lost." Instead, they are themselves visited by the one who is the Word and the bread. The Emmaus story shows us that it is Jesus who opens the scriptures and Jesus who places food into the hands of the disciples.

We might take this story as a mode for seeing the shape of worship as something we *receive* rather than something we *create*. The elements are simple: (1) the witness of the ancestors as we know them from the Scrip-tures, opened to us by what has been written, opened in the story by the presence of the Risen Christ, and (2) the meal whose bread is broken by the Risen One, whose brokenness is the vehicle through which our eyes, too, are opened. The elements are treasures given to the church by God's revelation. There is nothing newer than eyes being suddenly opened to wisdom and truth, to a vision that vanishes as soon as it is seen, to a mys-tery that has no ending. These are the gifts of word and sacrament. This should be great comfort because it offers to all people a means through which we might come together, listen, see, taste, and behold.

The Emmaus story challenges us to think about the possibility that Scrip-ture is telling us something about how we learn. This story does not say that the disciples understood the events in Jerusalem when the Scriptures were opened for them. No, it was only in the meal that they fully "got it." There is something about the ritual action, the gathering around the humanly manu-factured baked wheat food (wheat, at least, in that culture's experience) and the sharing of that bread that can fully make plain what Jesus meant about "Do this in remembrance of me." We do not "know" only with our brains. We also "know" with our bodies, with our hands and eyes, by sitting next to others who, with us, are preparing to eat some bread. The very primal act of gathering around food, intending to feed on what will give us another day of life, tells us something about Jesus, the bread of life.

Christians gather for worship in the name of God who created us and all that exists, who saves us daily from our own foolishness, and who inspires us by turning our fears into hope. We know this gracious God through the word that feeds us, brings us together, and creates commu-nity around a meal. God's word serves God's people by putting into our hearts and minds the promises of forgiveness and steadfast love through the song, prayer, and preaching in worship. Serving the word of God is what Christians are all about. It is our center and our journey.

Order of Service for the Case Study[1]

The Chapel of the Lutheran Theological Seminary at Philadelphia

Holy Communion
February 25, 2009 at 11:30 a.m.
Ash Wednesday

(Congregational responses are in bold)

Gathering	*The Holy Spirit calls us together as the people of God.*

The assembly gathers in silence.

Psalm 51
> *Congregation sings after each verse:*
> **Have mercy on me, O God, according to your steadfast love.**

Greeting   *ELW*, p. 251
> The Lord be with you.
> **And also with you.**

---

1. Excerpts from *Evangelical Lutheran Worship* (*ELW*) (Minneapolis: Augsburg Fortress, 2006), are copyright © 2006 Evangelical Lutheran Church in America. Used by permission. All rights reserved.

Prayer of the Day   *ELW*, p. 251
> Gracious God, out of your love and mercy you breathed into dust the breath
> of life, creating us to serve you and our neighbors. Call forth our prayers and
> acts of kindness, and strengthen us to face our mortality with confidence in
> the mercy of your son, Jesus Christ, our Savior and Lord, who lives and reigns
> with you and the Holy Spirit, one God, now and forever.
> **Amen.** [Ash Wednesday, *ELW*, p. 26]

Word   *God speaks to us in Scripture reading, preaching, and song.*

First Reading   *Return to God*   Joel 2:1-2, 12:17

Psalm 103:8-14 (sung)   *ELW*, #103

Second Reading   *Now is the day of salvation*   2 Corinthians 5:20b—6:10

Gospel Acclamation (Lent [sung])   *ELW*, p. 151
> **Return to the Lord, your God, for he is gracious and merciful, slow to
> anger and abounding in steadfast love.**

Gospel   *The practice of faith*   Matthew 6:1-6, 16-21

Sermon   Melinda Quivik
> [for sermon text, see above, pp. 42—46]

Hymn of the Day
> *Out of the Depths I Cry to You*   *ELW*, #600

Invitation to Lent   *ELW*, p. 252

Confession of Sin   *ELW*, p. 252
> Let us confess our sin in the presence of God and of one another.

> Most holy and merciful God,
> **we confess to you and to one another,**
> **and before the whole community of heaven,**
> **that we have sinned by our fault,**
> **by our own fault,**

by our own most grievous fault,
in thought, word, and deed,
by what we have done and by what we have left undone.

We have not loved you with our whole heart, and mind, and strength. We have not loved our neighbors as ourselves. We have not forgiven others as we have been forgiven.
Have mercy on us, O God.

We have shut our ears to your call to serve as Christ served us. We have not been true to the mind of Christ. We have grieved your Holy Spirit.
Have mercy on us, O God.

Our past unfaithfulness, the pride, envy, hypocrisy, and apathy that have infected our lives, we confess to you.
Have mercy on us, O God.

Our self-indulgent appetites and ways, and our exploitation of other people, we confess to you.
Have mercy on us, O God.

Our neglect of human need and suffering, and our indifference to injustice and cruelty, we confess to you.
Have mercy on us, O God.

Our false judgments, our uncharitable thoughts toward our neighbors, and our prejudice and contempt toward those who differ from us, we confess to you.
Have mercy on us, O God.

Our waste and pollution of your creation, and our lack of concern for those who come after us, we confess to you.
Have mercy on us, O God.

Restore us, O God, and let your anger depart from us.
Have mercy on us, O God.

Imposition of Ashes   *ELW*, p. 254
> *As the minister puts ashes on each forehead, these Words are said:*
> Remember that you are dust, and to dust you will return.

> *During the imposition, we sing in chant:*
> **Bless the Lord, my soul, and bless God's holy name.**
> **Bless the Lord, my soul, who leads me into life.**

> *Dialog after the imposition:*
> Accomplish in us, O God, the work of your salvation.
> **that we may show forth your glory in the world.**
> By the cross and passion of your Son, our Savior,
> **bring us with all your saints to the joy of his resurrection.**

> *The presiding minister addresses the assembly:*
> Almighty God have mercy on us, forgive us all our sins through our Lord Jesus
> Christ, strengthen us in all goodness, and by the power of the Holy Spirit keep
> us in eternal life.
> **Amen.**

Prayers of Intercession
> [See Appendix 2, p. 89, below.]

Passing of the Peace
> The peace of Christ be with you always.
> **And also with you.**

Meal   *God feeds us with the presence of Jesus Christ.*

Setting the Table
> *Softly and Tenderly Jesus is Calling*   *ELW* #608

Great Thanksgiving (sung)   *ELW*, pp. 152–54
> The Lord be with you.
> **And also with you.**
> Lift up your hearts.
> **We lift them to the Lord.**
> Let us give thanks to the Lord our God.
> **It is right to give our thanks and praise.**

**Holy, holy, holy Lord, Lord God of pow'r and might
heav'n and earth are full of your glory.
Hosanna in the highest.
Blessed is he who comes in the name of the Lord.
Hosanna in the highest.**
Blessed are you, O God of the universe.
Your mercy is everlasting and your faithfulness endures from age to age.
Praise to you for creating the heavens and the earth.
Praise to you for saving the earth from the waters of the flood.
Praise to you for bringing the Israelites safely through the sea.
Praise to you for leading your people through the wilderness to the land of milk and honey.
Praise to you for the words and deeds of Jesus, your anointed one.
Praise to you for the death and resurrection of Christ.
Praise to you for your Spirit poured out on all nations.

In the night in which he was betrayed, our Lord Jesus took bread and gave thanks; broke it; and gave it to his disciples, saying: Take and eat, this is my body, given for you. Do this for the remembrance of me.

Again, after supper, he took the cup, gave thanks, and gave it to all to drink, saying: This cup is the new covenant in my blood, shed for you and for all people for the forgiveness of sin. Do this for the remembrance of me.

With this bread and cup we remember our Lord's passover from death to life as we proclaim the mystery of faith:
**Christ has died.
Christ is risen.
Christ will come again.**

O God of resurrection and new life:
Pour out your Holy Spirit upon us and on these gifts of bread and wine.
Bless this feast.
Grace our table with your presence.
Come, Holy Spirit.

Reveal yourself to us in the breaking of the bread.
Raise us up as the body of Christ for the world.
Breathe new life into us.
Send us forth, burning with justice, peace, and, love.
Come, Holy Spirit.

With your holy ones of all times and places,
with the earth and all its creatures,
with sun and moon and stars,
we praise you, O God,
blessed and holy Trinity,
now and forever.
Amen. [Prayer IV, *ELW*, p. 111]

> **Our Father in heaven,**
> **hallowed be your name,**
> **your kingdom come,**
> **your will be done,**
> **on earth as in heaven.**
> **Give us today our daily bread.**
> **Forgive us our sins**
> **as we forgive those**
> **who sin against us.**
> **Save us from the time of trial**
> **and deliver us from evil.**
> **For the kingdom, the power,**
> **and the glory and yours,**
> **now and forever. Amen.**

Come to the banquet, for all is now ready.

Communion
Lamb of God   *ELW*, p. 154
Come Down, O Love Divine   *ELW*, #804
Once We Sang and Danced   *ELW*, #701

Prayer after Communion   *ELW,* p. 254

Merciful God, accompany our journey through these forty days. Renew us in
the gift of baptism, that we may provide for those who are poor, pray for those
in need, fast from self-indulgence, and above all that we may find our treasure
in the life of your Son, Jesus Christ, our Savior and Lord, who lives and reigns
with you and the Holy Spirit, one God, now and forever.

Amen.

Sending   *God blesses us and sends us in mission to the world.*

Blessing   *ELW,* p. 255

Almighty God, Father, + Son, and Holy Spirit, bless you now and forever.

Amen.

Sending Song:

Eternal Lord of Love, Behold Your Church   *ELW,* #321

Dismissal   *ELW,* p. 255

Go forth into the world to serve God with gladness;

be of good courage;

hold fast to that which is good;

render to no one evil for evil;

strengthen the fainthearted; support the weak;

help the afflicted; honor all people;

love and serve God, rejoicing in the power of the Holy Spirit.

Thanks be to God.

Intercessions for Ash Wednesday

What follows are the intercessions offered during the Ash Wednesday service described in this book, and may serve as an example to preachers and worship leaders (congregational responses are in boldface).

With the whole people of God in Christ Jesus,
Let us pray for the church, those in need, and all of God's creation.

Holy God, you whose Word is a daily joy to us,
we give you thanks for the church:
for all people who speak your word in our ears, open our eyes,
        and show us the Way,
for problem solvers, policy makers, rebels, prophets, poets, musicians,
        and artists of all kinds,
for people who teach and people in whom we see your face . . .
        Bless we the Lord / **Thanks be to God**.

We give you thanks for this fine earth:
for trees and shrubs, grasses, fruits and vegetables,
for all the animals, insects and fish,
for air, water, soil, wind, summer and autumn,
for those who defend the creatures who cannot speak to us,
for those who teach the way of respect for your creation . . .
        Bless we the Lord / **Thanks be to God**.

We give you thanks for the shifting changes in our lives:
for the goodness of our successes and the learning in our setbacks, for
        peace and for struggle, for times of rejoicing and for waiting in silence,

for repentance and forgiveness,
for all the ways you show us the path you have set out before us . . .
Bless we the Lord / **Thanks be to God**.

We beg your help this day, O God, for all the world:
for students beginning and returning to studies, especially here in Philadelphia,
for farmers and ranchers, people who fish and hunt,
those who live in cities and in villages, rainforests and deserts,
for prisoners, scientists, politicians, bureaucrats, and children,
for those who vote and those too cynical to be involved,
for the nations doing well and for those that are in jeopardy,
for the people of Iraq, Zimbabwe, Myanmar, China, Cuba, and Georgia,
for those wrongly imprisoned and those who work for justice . . .
Hear us, O God / **Your mercy is great.**

We beg your healing and peace on all who are in need:
for the sick, for those awaiting surgery,
for those in the midst of difficult decisions,
for families torn apart,
for all who do not believe that you, our Creator, know and love them,
for all who have been abused, shunned, denied self-love,
for everyone who is grieving . . .
Hear us, O God / **Your mercy is great.**

We bring before you now all else that lies upon our hearts . . . spoken and silent . . .
Hear us, O God / **Your mercy is great.**

We give thanks for the life, pastoral and political convictions, teaching, and hymnody of your servant Nicolai Grundtvig . . .
and for all your saints on whose witness we depend day after day.
Make us grateful. Teach us peace.

Into your hands, gracious God, we commend all for whom we pray, trusting in your mercy; through Jesus Christ, our Savior.
Amen.

Notes

Introduction

1. Gordon W. Lathrop, *Holy Things: A Liturgical Theology* (Minneapolis: Fortress Press, 1993), 15.

2. Nicholas Carr, "Is Google Making Us Stupid?" in *Atlantic Monthly* 301, no. 6 (July–August 2008), http://www.theatlantic.com/doc/200807/google, accessed June 17, 2009.

3. See Frank C. Senn, *The People's Work: A Social History of the Liturgy* (Minneapolis: Fortress Press, 2006), 23–24; The New Testament Greek Lexicon, http://www.studylight.org/lex/grk/view.cgi?number=3009, accessed April 6, 2009; and Louis H. Feldman, *Jew and Gentile in the Ancient World: Attitudes and Interactions from Alexander to Justinian* (Princeton: Princeton University Press, 1993), 159–60.

Chapter 1 • God's Word Is Central In Worship

1. See also Eph. 4:12, 16: "building up the body of Christ" and [the church] "building itself up in love."

2. Anne Lamott, *Traveling Mercies: Some Thoughts on Faith* (New York: Pantheon, 1999).

3. Aaron Milavec, ed., *The Didache: Text, Translation, Analysis, and Commentary* (Collegeville, Minn.: Liturgical, 2003).

4. Justin Martyr, *First Apology* in *Patrologiae Cursus Completus, Series Graeca*, ed. J.-P. Migne, vol. 6 (Paris, 1857), 420–32.

5. Lucien Deiss, C.S.Sp., *Springtime of the Liturgy: Liturgical Texts of the First Four Centuries* (Collegeville, Minn.: Liturgical, 1979), 121–54.

6. Milavec, ed., *The Didache*, ix.

7. Ibid., 19.

8. Ibid., 21.

9. Deiss, *Springtime of the Liturgy*, 93; see also Gordon Lathrop, *Central Things* (Minneapolis: Augsburg Fortress, 2005), 79.

10. Paul Bradshaw, ed., *New Westminster Dictionary of Liturgy and Worship* (Louisville: Westminster John Knox, 2002), 384.

11. Augustine, *The Confessions*, Book 1, Chapter 1 (London: Penguin, 1961), 21.

12. See the "Nairobi Statement on Worship and Culture: Contemporary Challenges and Opportunities," at http://www.worship.ca/docs/lwf_ns.html, accessed April 6, 2009.

13. Ibid., section 5.

Chapter 2 • Serving a Pattern

1. Martin Luther, *Formula Missae*, in *Liturgy and Hymns, Luther's Works*, vol. 53 (hereafter *LW*), trans. Paul Zeller Strodach and Ulrich S. Leupold (Philadelphia: Fortress Press, 1965), 20.

2. The ordo is not to be mistaken for the "order" of worship. The ordo is, rather, the large pattern of paradoxical symbols around which the assembly gathers for worship.

3. *LW* 53:25.

4. *LW* 53:19.

5. *LW* 53:80.

6. John Calvin, "Articles Concerning the Organization of the Church and of Worship at Geneva Proposed by the Ministers at the Council January 1, 1537," trans. J. K. S. Reid, in *Library of Christian Classics, Vol. XXII: Calvin: Theological Treatises* (Philadelphia: Westminster, 1954), 54.

7. John Calvin, *Institutes of the Christian Religion, Vol. I: 3.2.6*, trans. John Allen (Philadelphia: Presbyterian Board of Publication, 1813), 494.

8. *A Directory for the Publique Worship of God* (London, 1644), copy in University Library, Cambridge, 9–38, as quoted in James F. White, *Documents of Christian Worship* (Louisville: Westminster John Knox, 1992), 108–10.

9. A hymn sung before the sermon prepares the assembly to be open to hearing the word preached. For some Presbyterians, this is a Hymn of Illumination. For Baptists and others, the hymn in this place in the liturgy invokes the Holy Spirit on the preacher for preaching and on the assembly for hearing.

10. White, *Documents*, 109.

11. Ibid., 110.

12. B. W. Gorham, *Camp Meeting Manual: A Practical Book for the Camp Ground* (Boston: H.V. Degan, 1854), 155–56, as quoted in ibid., 111.

13. Faith and Order Commission, *Baptism, Eucharist, and Ministry* (Geneva: World Council of Churches, 1982), preface. The document can be found at http://www.oikoumene.org/?id=2638, accessed April 16, 2009.

14. Thomas F. Best and Dagmar Heller, *So We Believe, So We Pray: Towards Koinonia in Worship—The Ditchingham Report* (Geneva: World Council of Churches, 1995), http://www.oikoumene.org/en/resources/documents/wcc-commissions/faith-and-order, accessed April 16, 2009 (hereafter Ditchingham).

15. The consultation included Roman Catholic, Anglican, Presbyterian, Baptist, Eastern Orthodox, Lutheran, United, Mar Thoma, Disciples of Christ, and Methodist representatives from all over the world.

16. Full communion status means that denominations agree to hold the meal together despite theological differences over its meaning.

17. Ditchingham, II.18.

18. Ditchingham, IV.39.ii.

19. Ditchingham, IV.39.vi.

20. Ditchingham, IV.41.ii.b.

21. This label, "liturgical churches," is a misnomer if, by the word *liturgical* we refer to its Greek meaning, which had to do with a public event. Note: the use of the word as meaning "work of the people" needs more nuance than it usually receives. To call liturgy something "the people" do means to stresses the participation of the whole assembly. In fact, a liturgy in the ancient world was, like the Sunday liturgical event today, an open, public occurrence, but it was more a political event that furthered the status of the powerful at the expense of the rabble. This is not what Christian liturgy is about.

22. Dagmar Heller, "Ecumenical Worship," in Bradshaw, *New Westminster Dictionary* (Louisville: Westminster John Knox, 2002), 164.

23. Ditchingham, I.4.6.

24. ELLC today includes churches in Australia, New Zealand, Great Britain, Canada, and members in ICEL.

25. Conversation with Walter Brueggemann at an Asheville, North Carolina, preaching conference, Montreat Conference Center, June, 2000.

26. Philip Melanchthon, "The Apology of the Augsburg Confession," in Robert Kolb and Timothy J. Wengert, eds., *The Book of Concord* (Minneapolis: Fortress Press, 2000), 131.67.

27. Martin Luther, "The Large Catechism," in ibid., 436.38, 45.

28. Use of the RCL and of common liturgical texts—especially the Lord's Prayer, Apostle's and Nicene Creeds, blessings and collects or prayers of the day—is worldwide, embracing Anglican, Uniting, Presbyterian, Lutheran, Methodist, Roman Catholic, and Reformed churches in all continents. In North America, current CCT members include the Anglican Church of Canada, Canadian Conference of Catholic Bishops, Disciples of Christ, Christian Reformed, Church of the Brethren, Episcopal, Evangelical Lutheran, American Baptist Fellowship for Liturgical Renewal, Lutheran Church—Missouri Synod, Mennonite Church, National Conference of Catholic Bishops of the U.S., Polish National Catholic Church, Presbyterian Church (U.S.A.), Presbyterian Church in Canada, Reformed, Unitarian Universalist, United Church of Canada, United Church of Christ, and United Methodist.

Chapter 3 • Ash Wednesday: A Case Study

1. I do not consider the psalm a text to be mined for thematic sermonic material because its use as a hymn the assembly sings after the first reading places it in the category of being a response or a prayer. Use of a psalm phrase in the Ash Wednesday sermon simply employs imagery from the psalm as an echo to underscore the themes that arise out of the three readings.

2. Each year will necessarily have somewhat different emphases because Year A is based in Matthew, B in Mark, and C in Luke.

3. Because a sermon is truly an "oral" event, it is very difficult to translate a lively word to written form and have it sound at all the same. I have, therefore, left the layout in the pattern I use for preaching so that, at least, the breaks in phrasing—used for emphasis and pacing—can help the reader hear with the eye.

4. A full worship bulletin for the service at which this sermon was preached may be found in Appendix 1, p. 82.

Chapter 4 • Gathering

1. The calendar of festival and ordinary time kept by the ecumenical church may be called the liturgical year or church calendar or the church year. They all refer to the cycle of seasons that follow Jesus' birth, life, death, and resurrection and then the founding of the Christian church.

2. *Book of Common Worship* (Louisville: Westminster John Knox, 1993), 48–50 (hereafter *BCW*).

3. Mark Mummert, "Musical Power: Broken to the Center," in Timothy J. Wengert, ed., *Centripetal Worship: The Evangelical Heart of Lutheran Worship*, Worship Matters (Minneapolis: Augsburg Fortress, 2007), 35–36.

4. In *Evangelical Lutheran Worship* (Minneapolis: Augsburg Fortress, 2006), these are hymn ##853, 520, 528, 526, and 821, respectively (hereafter *ELW*).

5. It is important to remember in choosing hymns that the assembly should not be faced with only unfamiliar hymns on a given Sunday. Some hymns, while thematically appropriate, are difficult to sing and might best be used first as a solo or a choir anthem. Hymns for assembly singing must be readily grasped or deliberately taught. A new hymn needs time to be taught and digested. The musician, choir director, or cantor might introduce the tune over several weeks, beginning by simply playing the melody before worship, then having the children sing it during the offering, leading the congregation through it before worship on a Sunday, and finally appointing it as an assembly hymn. People retain tunes quite readily when they have been played several times. After learning a new hymn, the assembly should be allowed to sing it several times over several weeks.

6. *The Book of Common Prayer* (New York: Church Hymnal Corp., 1928), 227.

7. Found in, for instance, *ELW*, #326.

8. An alternative Ash Wednesday Prayer of the Day is this, also offered in *ELW* (p. 26): "Almighty and ever-living God, you hate nothing you have made, and you forgive the sins of all who are penitent. Create in us new and honest hearts, so that, truly repenting of our sins, we may receive from you, the God of all mercy, full

pardon and forgiveness through your son, Jesus Christ, our Savior and Lord, who lives and reigns with you and the Holy Spirit, one God, now and forever. Amen."

Chapter 5 • Word

1. O. Wesley Allen, *Preaching and Reading the Lectionary: A Three-Dimensional Approach to the Liturgical Year* (St. Louis: Chalice, 2007).

2. An apocryphal reading or a passage from Acts (especially during the Easter season) may be read for the first reading.

3. Melinda and Fredric Quivik, "Writing Prayers for Sunday Worship," in *Sundays and Seasons* (Minneapolis: Augsburg Fortress, 2005), 13–14.

4. A very detailed Lenten fasting discipline is available on the Web site of the Orthodox Church in America at http://www.oca.org/OCFasting.asp?SID=2, accessed April 8, 2009.

5. Found in, for instance, *ELW*, ##793, 801.

6. Ibid., ##626, 358.

7. Ibid., #600.

8. Ibid., #701.

9. An example of intercessions appropriate to Ash Wednesday may be found in Appendix 2, p. 89.

Chapter 6 • Meal

1. Aaron Milavec, ed., *The Didache: Text, Translation, Analysis, and Commentary* (Collegeville, Minn.: Liturgical, 2003), 23–25.

2. Found in, for instance, *ELW*, #608.

3. See Eucharistic Prayer IV for Ash Wednesday in *ELW*, p. 111.

4. Found in, for instance, *ELW*, #804.

Chapter 7 • Sending

1. Thomas Schattauer, ed., "Liturgical Assembly as Locus of Mission," in *Inside-Out: Worship in an Age of Mission* (Minneapolis: Fortress Press, 1999), 1–22.

2. Clayton J. Schmit, *Sent and Gathered: A Worship Manual for the Missional Church* (Grand Rapids: Baker Academic, forthcoming, 2009).

3. *ELW*, 115.

4. *BCW*, p. 161; based on Rom. 15:13.

5. Ibid., p. 159; based on Matt. 22:37-30.

6. Ibid., p. 160; based on Col. 3:12-14.

7. Found, for instance, in *ELW*, #321.

For Further Reading

Byars, Ronald. *The Future of Protestant Worship: Beyond the Worship Wars.* Louisville: Westminster John Knox, 2002.

Childers, Jana, and Clayton J. Schmit. *Performance in Preaching: Bringing the Sermon to Life.* Grand Rapids: Baker Academic, 2008.

Chupungco, Anscar J. *Liturgical Inculturation: Sacramentals, Religiosity, and Catechesis.* Collegeville: Liturgical, 1992.

Costen, Melva Wilson. *African American Christian Worship.* Nashville: Abingdon, 2007.

Greenhaw, David M., and Ronald J. Allen. *Preaching in the Context of Worship.* St. Louis: Chalice, 2000.

Lathrop, Gordon W. *The Pastor: A Spirituality.* Minneapolis: Fortress Press, 2006.

Lischer, Richard. *The End of Words: The Language of Reconciliation in a Culture of Violence.* Grand Rapids: Eerdmans, 2005.

Moore-Keish, Martha L. *Do This in Remembrance of Me: A Ritual Approach to Reformed Eucharistic Theology.* Grand Rapids: Eerdmans, 2008.

Ramshaw, Gail. *A Three-Year Banquet: The Lectionary for the Assembly.* Worship Matters. Minneapolis: Augsburg Fortress, 2004.

———. *Treasures Old and New: Images in the Lectionary.* Minneapolis: Fortress Press, 2002.

Rice, Charles L. *The Embodied Word: Preaching as Art and Liturgy.* Minneapolis: Fortress Press, 1990.

Schlafer, David J. *What Makes This Day Different? Preaching Grace on Special Occasions.* Cambridge: Cowley, 1998.

Searle, Mark. *Called to Participate; Theological, Ritual, and Social Perspectives.* Collegeville: Liturgical, 2006.